Lesson-drawing in Public Policy
A Guide to Learning across Time and Space

Richard Rose
Centre for the Study of Public Policy
University of Strathclyde

The real world in fact is perhaps the most fertile of all sources of good research questions calling for basic scientific inquiry.

— Herbert A. Simon, Nobel laureate lecture

Chatham House Publishers, Inc.
Chatham, New Jersey

Lesson-drawing in Public Policy Chatham House Publishers, Inc.
A Guide to Learning across   Post Office Box One
Time and Space   Chatham, New Jersey 07928

Copyright © 1993 by Chatham House Publishers, Inc.

All rights reserved. No part of this publication may be reproduced, stored on a retrieval system, or transmitted in any form or by any means, electronic, mechanical, photocopying, recording, or otherwise without prior permission of the publisher.

PUBLISHER: Edward Artinian
PRODUCTION SUPERVISOR: Katharine Miller
COVER DESIGN: Antler & Baldwin Design Group, Inc.
COMPOSITION: Bang, Motley, Olufsen
PRINTING AND BINDING: A to Z Printing

Library of Congress Cataloging-in-Publication Data

Rose, Richard, 1933–
  Lesson-drawing in public policy : a guide to learning across time and space / Richard Rose.
    p.   cm.
  Includes bibliographical references and index.
  ISBN 0-934540-32-2
  I . Policy sciences. I. Title.
H97.R666   1993   92-36205
                                                            CIP

Manufactured in the United States of America
10 9 8 7 6 5 4 3 2 1

*Dedicated to Mrs. Bemis,
who first taught me about space*

Contents

1. Learning from Experience—Consciously and Unconsciously 1
   Varieties of Experience. Proceeding to Learn.

2. What Is Lesson-drawing? 19
   Defining a Lesson. Drawing a Lesson. Is Lesson-drawing Possible? The Need to Be Doubly Desirable.

3. Searching for Lessons 50
   Who Searches? Dissatisfaction: the Stimulus to Search. Informal and Formal Sources of Ideas. Evaluating Lessons across Time and Space.

4. Searching across Time 77
   Obstacles to Searching the Past. Learning from One's Own Past. Unbounded Speculation about the Future.

5. Searching across Space 95
   Searching within a National System. Searching within a Permeable International System. Bridging Time and Space: Their Present, Our Future.

6. Contingencies of Lesson-drawing 118
   Uniqueness of Programs. Institutions as Necessary Means. Resources as a Constraint. Complexity of Programs. Scale of Change. Impact of Interdependence. Values Shape Ends.

7. Time Turns Obstacles into Variables 143
   Responding to Changing Contingencies. As Time Goes By.

References, 159
Index, 172
About the Author, 176

Figures and Tables

Figures

2.1	Desirability and Practicality of Transferring Programs	46
3.1	Evaluation across Time and Space	72
5.1	Consistency in Adoption of Conservative or Liberal Social Programs	103
5.2	International Telephone Calls	106
5.3	Differences in Values and Resources among OECD Nations	109
5.4	East European Desire to Learn from the West	111
6.1	Fungibility of Innovative Programs	121
7.1	Responses to Changes in the Policy Environment	146

Tables

2.1	Alternative Ways of Drawing a Lesson	30
2.2	Sources of Lessons in Meiji Japan	43
3.1	Differences of Opinion among British Economists	67
3.2	Health Program Outputs and Outcomes	75
5.1	Information Sources of Innovative State Officials	101
5.2	Country That East Europeans Most Want to Be Like	114
6.1	Differences between Simple and Complex Programs	133

Preface

Students of public policy usually learn lessons by reading books; policymakers usually learn lessons from experience. Learning from books is usually considered theoretical, and learning from experience, practical. Even though the two modes of learning are very different, the one need not exclude the other, for theories can lead to practical prescriptions, and maxims drawn from experience can epitomize the message of a theory.

Lesson-drawing is practical; it is concerned with making policy prescriptions that can be put into effect. Lessons are not learned in order to pass examinations; they are tools for action. Politicians know what they would like to achieve, but the existence of a political majority for a goal is no assurance that politicians will know how to design a program that achieves this goal. Borrowing a program that is effective elsewhere is no guarantee of success. Understanding under what circumstances and to what extent programs effective elsewhere will work here is an essential element in lesson-drawing.

Lessons can be positive, leading to prescriptions about what ought to be done. As health policy analyst Alain C. Enthoven (1990: 58) explains, "The really interesting questions are how to identify and design politically feasible incremental changes in each country that have a reasonably good chance of making things better. Each country can get useful ideas from others about how to do this." Lessons can also be negative; examples of failure identify what *not* to emulate. As Mikhail Gorbachev said after the collapse of Soviet communism, "That model has failed which was brought about in our country. And I hope that this is a lesson not only for our people but for all peoples" (quoted in Lichfield, 1991).

Lesson-drawing is normative insofar as a prescription to adopt a measure drawn from another is a statement about what ought to be done. Since politics is the expression of conflicting views about what government ought to do, a lesson can be controversial and stimulate opposition from those who object to the lesson's means or goal.

Lesson-drawing has a theoretical element, too. Concepts are required to generalize from experience in two different places and to formulate hypotheses about whether a program can effectively transfer from one place to another (Rose, 1991a). The concepts and hypotheses implicit or explicit in lesson-drawing are generic, that is, applicable in principle to many places. As the term is used here, a lesson is more than a historian's case study; it refers to problems found in at least two different societies.

Lesson-drawing bridges both time and space. The time dimension is necessarily a part of lesson-drawing, for policymakers search for lessons that will alter what they do in the future. The time dimension is present whether policymakers search their own past for lessons of what worked before or seek to evaluate whether a lesson drawn from current experience elsewhere will improve their own government in the future.

Searching for lessons across space is a practice known to America's Founding Fathers. They conscientiously studied the British constitution to learn how to avoid faults of governance that led them to revolt against the Crown. Today, American federalism is often characterized as a laboratory for experiment. A program developed in one state or city can be examined by other cities or states for lessons about how to improve policies. In an increasingly open environment, policymakers dissatisfied with their present performance can seek lessons from programs that appear to bring satisfaction elsewhere.

Lesson-drawing involves a return to the original idea of social science, which was both comparative and theoretical. Aristotle was not an "Agora-watcher," the Athenian equivalent of a White House-watcher in Washington. Instead, Aristotle observed differences in the ways in which states responded to common problems of governance in order to arrive at general propositions for improving the governance of Athens. "For many classical writers, the notion of comparative sociological study would sound redundant. Sociology *had to be* comparative" (Nowak, 1989:34; italics in the original).

OBJECT OF THE BOOK

The purpose is to provide a guide to drawing lessons about public policy. The book is a guide because it introduces readers to a novel way of thinking about familiar problems of public policy. It sets out the crucial questions that must be asked in order to draw logical and empirically sound conclusions from observing experience in the past, or in other places. Even in a jet age, there is nothing wrong with suggesting that the policymakers should be able to walk through the steps necessary to learn from experience before they rush to the airport.

Although policymakers invariably engage in lesson-drawing, they do so unselfconsciously. As subsequent pages show, the so-called "lessons" of history are at worst factually incorrect and at best disputed by historians. The "lessons" of one man or woman's experience may be contradicted by the experience of colleagues —or even by other maxims that an individual is fond of quoting. The emphasis here is not on explaining how learning occurs. Instead, it is on selecting social science concepts that can give readers guidance in drawing lessons from the everyday actions of governments, and on evaluating critically policy prescriptions based on what are claimed to be "proven lessons" from other times and places.

The issue is not whether we draw lessons from experience, but whether we do so well or badly. One response is to deny that we can learn anything from the experience of any place else. Programs that demonstrably are in effect elsewhere are said to be incapable of being transferred: "They are different because they are there, not here." This is the voice of parochialism or isolationism. Even though some American politicians believe that isolationism is popular and symbolically beat up foreigners, this is grandstanding, not policymaking. Bashing the Japanese on television or in the public print does not make Japan disappear, and smashing Japanese television sets on the steps of the United States Capitol does not make Americans stop buying Japanese television sets. The best way to achieve that goal is to emulate what the Japanese once did, namely, learn how to make the same set cheaper, or better.

More than a century ago the Japanese learned that even a nation insular in both culture and geography cannot live in isolation from other nations. Since the New Deal and, even more, since the Supreme Court decision on racial desegregation in 1954, Americans have learned that no city or state can ignore what happens in other parts of the United States, or what is done by the federal government. Today, as President Clinton has emphasized, policymakers faced with nations that are both friends and competitors cannot afford to ignore lessons drawn from foreign experience.

ACKNOWLEDGMENTS

As is appropriate for a study that spans time and space, this book has been a long time in the making on two continents. My first political memories are of World War II; that was sufficient reminder that it is dangerous to ignore what is happening in other countries. An awareness of differences between peoples was cultivated in childhood in St. Louis; a long streetcar ride to the baseball park crossed very different parts of that metropolitan area. Studies and subsequent academic research led me to explore differences in forms of government across the United States, across Europe, and across continents farther afield. In these journeys I have often reflected on the differences observed and the extent to which it is possible to draw lessons for public policy from experience elsewhere.

Every American is raised with the belief that the United States is a vanguard nation, with lessons to teach other nations. Hence, it is appropriate that my first foray in lesson-drawing was an edited book, *Lessons from America* (Rose, 1974: especially 11ff), in which contributors dealt with subjects as varied as the American economy, advertising, social welfare programs, and architecture and design. American experience was said sometimes to offer Europeans positive lessons, and sometimes negative. The volume also cautioned against the confusion of actual practice with mythic visions of America (see also Rose, 1991b).

The uniqueness of the American presidency is an ambivalent attribute. It may be interpreted as evidence of the genius of American politics, or as the lack of certain attributes that are taken for granted in parliamentary systems with a prime minister. Editing a book on *Presidents and Prime Ministers* (Rose and Suleiman, 1980) in the last days of the Carter administration brought me up against the distinction between comparative analysis and lesson-drawing. Acting as a United Nations Development Program adviser to the president-elect of Colombia made me appreciate that, even in an unfamiliar country, there are general principles of politics from which lessons can be drawn (Rose, 1990a).

When the Spanish government was considering reform of the electoral laws in its nascent democracy, I was invited to give a paper in Madrid on what could be learned from the operation of electoral systems in other democracies. This was a stimulus to develop a generic framework for analyzing the variety of choices in electoral system and highlighting the lessons that could confidently be drawn about the consequences of adopting one system instead of another (Rose, 1983).

Collaborating with Japanese in editing a book, *The Welfare State East and West* (Rose and Shiratori, 1986), enabled me to experience firsthand the unusual combination of otherness and familiarity that Japan offers the world. Taken as a whole, Japanese culture seems different. Yet when one comes to grips with many of its public policies, similarities are substantial. This should not be surprising, for the Japanese were the first and most successful nation studying Western societies in order to "catch up" in public policy as in the economy.

The unwelcome rise in unemployment is a textbook example of a common problem facing policymakers in many lands. Given that levels and responses of government have differed, there is a strong case for seeking positive lessons from the experience of countries with low unemployment, a task that is harder to accomplish in practice than in theory, as even sophisticated econometric studies conclude (see, e.g., *Economica*, 1986). Given that German unemployment was substantially lower than that in Britain in the mid-1980s, I undertook a comparative analysis of the two countries, seeking to identify programs in effect in one country that might improve conditions in the other. This was supported by a grant from the Anglo-German Foundation, London, supplemented by the Wissenschaftszentrum Berlin.

The big discrepancy between the two countries arose from the fact that youth unemployment in Britain was very much higher than in Germany. The British government noticed this, too; it announced that it would emulate the German dual system of vocational and educational training. This created an unusual opportunity to examine lesson-drawing in action through systematic comparison of what Germany actually does with what the British government is proposing to do. An analytic model was developed to distinguish between the rhetoric of lesson-drawing—British policymakers claiming credit for achieving German standards in advance of the fact—and the reality: The British program is an infirm copy of what Germany actually does (see Rose and Wignanek, 1990; Prais, 1989). The use of lesson-drawing for prospective evaluation was demonstrated in a paper that showed that the "half-lesson" drawn by the British government might produce only one-tenth the promised results by the year 2000 (Rose, 1991c).

Since lesson-drawing involves a trial-and-error search across space and time, the study also highlighted one advantage that Britain enjoys vis-à-vis Germany, namely, much greater flexibility in adopting new programs and abandoning programs that appear to be failing. German policymakers are inhibited by rigidities arising from the legalistic framework of policymaking in the Federal Republic, an inhibition difficult to alter because it is embedded in the German constitution. A second inhibition is that German budgets tend to compartmentalize revenue and expenditure, so that costs and benefits are not reviewed together, whereas the British practice of comprehensive budgeting provides greater incentives to swap programs (Rose and Page, 1990: 76ff; cf. Schmid and Reissert, 1988). This British lesson for Germany, which could be adopted without constitutional amendment, has gained in significance as German unemployment has risen in the 1990s.

Preface

Sitting as a visiting professor in an office in the remains of an old Prussian building of the Wissenschaftszentrum Berlin (WZB), the largest social science research center in Europe, was a stimulus to think expansively and to produce the first draft of a systematic overview of lesson-drawing as a process. During my second sojourn, the fall of the Berlin Wall gave East Europeans the opportunity to learn from free societies and market economies. At the WZB, its president Professor Wolfgang Zapf, Bernd Reissert, Günther Schmid, Georg Thurn, and Günter Wignanek were good partners in discussion. Ideas herein were tried out in seminars at the Wissenschaftszentrum Berlin, Yale University, the University of Toronto, the United States Institute of Peace in Washington, D.C., and George Mason University.

To secure more grist for the mill, I organized a panel on lesson-drawing at the 1990 American Political Science Association meetings in San Francisco, at which papers were presented by Colin Bennett, George Hoberg, Giandomenico Majone, and David Brian Robertson, covering topics as diverse as environmental policy, regulation, social policy, and freedom of information. These papers, along with an article by myself containing analytic points referred to in chapters 1 and 2 of this book, have since appeared as a special issue of the *Journal of Public Policy* (Rose, 1991d).

The invitation to give four Ransone Lectures at the University of Alabama in 1990 encouraged making this a short book that provides a guide to a large subject, for lectures must concentrate on basic concepts and procedures of lesson-drawing. A short book can incorporate examples from my own writings, from the APSA panel, and from other authors without burying general points in a mass of details from case studies.

The subject of lesson-drawing is particularly appropriate to the South, for the Alabama lectures originated at the end of World War II to bring there a scholar who might contribute something to the improvement of public administration in a part of the United States that was then rural and poor. The lectures were delivered at the university's doctoral program of public administration at the Air University, Maxwell Air Force Base, in Montgomery. The audience had ground and air experience of many continents and outranked me militarily. The organizers of the Ransone Lectures—Victor Gibean and William Stewart at Tuscaloosa and Ann Riddle, Commander Robert Bushong, and Major Ray Conley at Montgomery—displayed the characteristic southern virtue of hospitality.

In my younger years as an academic I was fortunate in being stimulated to think about time and space by three great scholars, each very different yet combining imagination and detailed scholarly knowledge: Stein Rokkan, W.J.M. Mackenzie, and Gabriel Almond. As the citations to Herbert Simon show, his ideas have been important in establishing the foundations of this book. In writing it, I realized that having a father educated as a research engineer has also influenced my interest in how things work.

Helpful comments and criticisms were received from Colin Bennett, Lloyd Etheredge, William A. Glaser, Alexander George, Victor Gibean, Peter A. Hall, Theodore R. Marmor, David Brian Robertson, Paul Sabatier, Aaron Wildavsky, and two anonymous reviewers. None is responsible for any errors of omission or commission.

I

Learning from Experience— Consciously and Unconsciously

By my faith! For more than forty years I have been speaking prose without even suspecting it?

— Monsieur Jourdain in Molière's
Le Bourgeois Gentilhomme

Most policymakers draw lessons in an unreflective way; a lesson is no more than an assertion of "what everyone knows." President Bush is an extreme example of a policymaker who not only rejected the idea of having goals—the "vision thing"—but also preferred to concentrate on "the day-to-day things" in the belief that "if you do well in the short run, the long run will take care of itself." Relatively few policymakers are practiced in the logic of social science evaluation or comparative analysis. The evidence that politicians are looking for is a good fit between a prescription and the political interests of those drawing a lesson.

This book asks: What is it that intelligent people do without thinking? Generalization from experience is the essence of unselfconscious lesson-drawing. We draw lessons from our own past or from the experience of others in the same organization. When we travel, whether to another city or another country, both differences and similarities are noticed. Differences are a stimulus to seeking lessons about the way in which we order our activities at home. Just as Molière's upstart man of wealth could speak prose without ever having taken lessons, so everyone concerned with public policy unconsciously draws lessons across time and space.

The importance that policymakers give to experience derives from their concern with feasibility: Is a proposed policy capable of being carried out? Public officials have little interest in discussing measures that have never been put into effect. The experience of seeing a program in effect elsewhere demonstrates that it can be realized in at least one place.

Social scientists, by contrast, are self-conscious lesson-drawers, wanting to know the logic by which a lesson is drawn and the evidence indicating how a policy achieves its results. It is easy to use the tools of social science to challenge proposals based on a traveler's fleeting impressions and anecdotes. But pointing out the inadequacy of conclusions drawn from experience does not help policymakers.

A common experience of problems is the starting point in lesson-drawing. Often policymakers consider the problems of their particular jurisdiction as unique. Up to a point this is true, for every city has its own history, and every mayor a different electorate. Urban decay in Birmingham, Alabama, is a concern of the citizens of Birmingham, whereas decay in Detroit is a problem to people in Michigan. Differences can be greater still when comparisons are made across national boundaries separating Birmingham, Alabama, and Birmingham, England.

Yet the concerns that lead ordinary people to turn to government—education, safety on the streets, economic prosperity—are common across continents. Within a given field of public policy, much remains the same wherever one turns. Schools are expected to teach children to read and write whether the language of instruction is English or French or Japanese; the police are expected to prevent crime and maintain order whether they patrol a rural county, a suburb, or an inner city; and governments are expected to promote price stability and economic growth whatever the nation's currency. It is often easier to see similarities between the same policy area in different states or countries than to find similarities within a country between problems as different as education, policing, and managing the economy. Problems unique to one country, such as Watergate or German reunification, are the exception, not the rule.

Dissatisfaction with government is widespread, too. Everywhere policymakers are under pressure to act. Public officials can no longer rely on what was considered good enough in the past. The more intense the dissatisfaction, the greater the demand to do something. The question is, what to do? Lesson-drawing is one tool that policymakers can use when confronted with a situation that causes dissatisfaction.

Lesson-drawing from experience has two preconditions: easy access to information about what other governments are doing, and different responses to common problems. Both conditions are met within the United States, and internationally. Information about programs elsewhere is delivered daily to policymakers in the morning paper, in telephone calls and meetings, and by the evening television news. Policymakers are often free riders, acquiring information without cost from their everyday activities.

Within a federal system programs can vary in response to a common problem. There are thousands of towns and counties responsible for police protection, sanitation, and education, and tens of thousands of public officials working on new programs. A Ford Foundation project to publicize program innovations in state and local government annually receives more than 1000 nominations of new ways of solving old problems or dealing with new problems (Jordan, 1990). The programs range from computer-assisted reporting of crime through helping parents of very young children prepare for school.

Internationally, the flow of information about public policies has been radically accelerated by modern technology moving people and information from one continent to another. Washington, D.C., is now closer by plane to London or Bonn than it was to Chicago fifty years ago, and it is today closer to Tokyo than it then was to Los Angeles. International telephone and fax lines permit the instantaneous exchange of ideas across oceans, and their use is accelerating. In the decade from 1978 to 1988 the volume of international telephone calls increased by 500 percent to 30 billion minutes a year, and it is forecast to increase fivefold in the 1990s (Staple, 1990).

The variability of programs is greater across national boundaries than within a country. Differences in national resources and political values make it difficult or impossible to draw lessons that can be applied to the 160 different nations of the globe. Yet even if 90 percent are dismissed as "too different" from us to offer usable lessons, there remain more than a dozen advanced industrial nations that have the resources to develop sophisticated responses to common problems and to respond in sufficiently different ways to offer the possibility of learning by lesson-drawing.

In an era in which the average household contains goods from at least three continents—America, Europe, and Asia—public policies have also become part of the international flow of goods and services. In order to draw lessons, we must learn to position our actions in both time and space; that is the first topic of this chapter. So that readers can appreciate the variety of ways in which lesson-drawing is relevant to everyday concerns, the chapter then shows how functional concerns with topics as different as individual protection from computerized data bases, health care, unemployment, and environmental pollution have a lesson-drawing dimension. Lessons are not given in nature; they are tools designed for use by policymakers. Hence, the chapter describes ideas as "tools." Because every lesson addresses a specific problem, the use of this tool is contingent. Just as one must know whether to use a screwdriver or a hammer, so one must know what type of lesson is appropriate to a given context, or whether experience anywhere else is applicable to the problem at hand.

Varieties of Experience

Every policymaker can draw on two types of experience: his or her own knowledge of how programs operate, and the experience of others. Direct experience is easily subject to self-conscious examination, for when dissatisfaction arises, policymakers are under pressure to learn from their own mistakes. Although the relevance of one's own experience is immediate, its limits are also very real, for dissatisfaction indicates that an individual or agency may not be the best qualified to design a program that will be effective. When one's organization faces a problem common to many agencies, this is a stimulus to examine how others are responding.

GETTING BEARINGS IN TIME AND SPACE

To understand where we are at present, we must have bearings in both time and space. The average public official relies on routines established in the past to guide present actions. Standard operating procedures provide routine guidelines and sustain bureaucratic predictability. Routines also impose a narrow vision. As long as everything was satisfactory the last time anyone looked, there is no need to learn anything. Present experience reinforces past experience.

When structural change occurs, what worked before no longer works as it once did. For example, the role of the federal government in 1932, when Ronald Reagan was old enough to vote, differed fundamentally from 1989, when Reagan left the White House. Reagan could not return the federal government to the "normalcy" of Warren Harding and Calvin Coolidge. When structural changes are great, policymakers cannot expect lessons from the past to apply in the present.

At this point, policymakers are encouraged to search elsewhere in space. City officials can turn to officials in other cities in the same metropolitan area, in the same state, or in other states. State officials can turn to officials dealing with the same problem in other states. National officials may look to states and cities if they are responsible for programs administered there, such as housing or education. However, national officials responsible for programs that are the unique concern of national government, such as defense or diplomacy, must look to other nations.

Differences across space are increasingly matters of degree, not kind. Differences within a nation may be as great as differences between nations. Although Quebec and Saskatchewan are both provinces of Canada, their residents differ in language and culture. Much the same could be said about Minnesota and Louisiana, or

Massachusetts and New Mexico. Collective action by a dozen member states of the European Community shows that it is possible for separate countries to join together to adopt common policies. The distance between America and European countries is not so great as that between them and poor Third World nations.

Today, interdependence, not isolation, characterizes every jurisdiction of government; this is true of national governments as well as of state and local governments. Everywhere there is evidence of interdependence, such as the prices that motorists pay for gasoline and that farmers receive for corn and wheat. Even though the president sees himself as a global leader, most Washington policymakers are introverted. A "merchandiser of ideas" in the Washington policy community concludes:

> Unfortunately, creative and systematic international learning is an area in which U.S. activity and commitment trails its current—and up and coming—economic competitors. In the U.S. until recently, our nearly self-contained continental market and culture were the international success story. This very success makes our new task—the adaptation of state and local, public and private institutions—more challenging and difficult than for countries with a longer history of operating in an international context. (Heald, 1988: 13)

Policymakers who live in small countries subject to the influence of larger neighbors recognize that many decisions influencing them are taken elsewhere. Hence, the Canadian government watches what is done in Washington, and smaller European countries such as the Netherlands and Belgium watch what is done in Germany and France. Japan, a big country that has had a small-country complex, regularly sends domestic policy officials abroad in order to learn from the experience of Western nations.

Big nations can learn from the experience of other countries that have been quicker to adopt a program. For example, Britain did not have a value-added tax (VAT) on sales before joining the European Community in 1973. Adopting a value-added tax was a condition of entry; hence, tax collection officials faced the challenge of designing and implementing a major new tax in a short period of time. Before doing so the British government sent teams of four or five people to five different countries that had already adopted a value-added tax—France, Germany, the Netherlands, Denmark, and Sweden—in order to learn from their experience some of the practicalities and pitfalls of this complex tax. In the words of an official involved, "We brought back not only weighty bundles of VAT literature in foreign languages but also, thanks to the candid and helpful oral expositions we had had, the rudiments at least of an understanding of what the literature meant in practice and how VAT actually worked" (Johnstone, 1975: 21).

A FUNCTIONAL FOCUS

The great majority of policymakers are specialists, not generalists; their focus is on a functional set of problems, for example, education, transportation, or defense. This is true of members of Congress whose power base is in committees and subcommittees, of agency officials with a bureaucratically defined set of tasks, and of interest groups whose clients have very specific interests. A city sanitation officer is not interested in other cities for their own sake but in order to learn from their experience in dealing with sanitation problems; a state education official is concerned with how other states are dealing with education problems; and a national secretary of defense with the defense programs of other nations.

Lesson-drawing cuts across territorial boundaries but remains within the boundaries of a given policy community. Within a national system common functional concerns lead to a sharing of information between officials dealing with the same problem in different institutions of government. Politics unites what institutions divide. Today, common functional concerns also create opportunities for learning from the experience of other nations (Rose, 1988a: 233ff), as the following examples illustrate.

The worldwide development of large computers with data bases containing personal information about millions of persons illustrates how a common technological stimulus and concern with the goal of protecting privacy can stimulate learning across space. The enactment of data protection acts at different points in time, starting in Sweden in 1973 and the United States in 1974, provides a well-documented example of vicarious learning across national boundaries, for those countries adopting legislation later could and usually did examine the experience of the early adopters before drafting their own national legislation (see Bennett, 1988a; 1988b).

The technology of computing is such that data bases are assembled by the same principles and often by the same computer programs in many countries. Policymakers have similar goals: preventing disclosure of personal information without an individual's prior consent; allowing individuals access to information about themselves and the right to make corrections of inaccuracies; and the avoidance of secrecy in the compilation of data bases about individuals. There soon developed "a fairly coherent network of legal experts ... that read each others' reports and kept in constant contact with technological and legal developments" (Bennett, 1990: 562). The transmission of knowledge about what was happening in other countries was also promoted by transnational pressure groups, such as computer manufacturers, which desired harmonious or standard policies so that their wares could be built and operate in the same way in different countries. Even though national legal systems created differences in the particular mechanisms by which the protection of privacy was realized, commonalities in programs reflect conscious lesson-drawing as well.

Health care is a common concern in every country, too. There is a broad consensus about goals: Everyone wants to be in good health, and no one wants to be denied life-saving treatment because of a lack of money. Every country devotes a substantial amount of its gross national product to paying for health care. There are substantial differences between countries in the relative importance of public spending versus private spending for health care, and in the programs that determine the specific forms of health care. Hence, policymakers dissatisfied with present performance can expect to learn about different ways of formulating health policies by examining experience in other countries. There are also sufficient commonalities in the technology of medical and hospital treatment to create many similarities in the supply of and demand for health care.

Learning from Experience—Consciously and Unconsciously

In the United States there is widespread dissatisfaction with the high cost of health care. Americans devote more than half again as much to health expenditure as does the average advanced nation. Yet in infant mortality the United States ranks in the bottom quarter of advanced industrial nations, and in life expectancy it ranks in the middle, not at the top (see table 3.2). There is ample information available about the variety of health programs in effect in other countries, and some scholars specialize in comparisons that draw explicit lessons for American health programs (see, e.g., Glaser, 1987, 1988; Marmor, 1983: chapter 5).

However, in the absence of a political consensus about what ought to be done and who ought to pay the cost of changes in health programs, lessons are learned but not applied. The former surgeon general, Dr. C. Everett Koop (1990), even questions whether the United States has anything to learn from the superior performance of other nations, denouncing a "growing infatuation in the United States with health care systems in other countries."

The rise in unemployment in advanced industrial nations shows that the existence of a common problem is insufficient to call forth a solution, notwithstanding the fact that countries adopt different programs at the same point in time and vary their own programs across time. In the past two decades the average level of unemployment has almost tripled among advanced industrial nations, and every nation has experienced one or more major upsurges in the rate of unemployment. Given the political dissatisfaction caused by rising unemployment, policymakers have been anxious to find programs that will respond positively to this problem.

There has been active cross-national searching for programs to cope with rising unemployment. A team of American officials travels to Britain, France, and Germany in order to prepare a report entitled *Lessons from Europe* (Carlson et al., 1986). A French team concerned with creating jobs travels in the opposite direction in order to write a report entitled *Lessons from the United States* (Dommergues et al., 1989). The Organization for Economic Cooperation and Development (OECD) actively disseminates "best practice" ideas from its continuous monitoring of national employment programs and also seeks to assist local and regional governments to learn lessons through a project on Local Initiatives for Employment.

However, the absence of intellectual consensus among economists makes it difficult for policymakers to draw lessons with confidence from the experience of other countries. Nobel laureates in economics disagree with each other about whether unemployment reflects faults in government's control of the money supply or failure to apply Keynesian prescriptions to stimulate demand. There are disagreements about whether unemployment reflects supply-side structural weaknesses or demand-side cyclical problems. There are also disagreements about whether government ought to or can alter the level of unemployment, and whether reducing unemployment or other policy goals, such as reducing inflation, should have the highest priority. Disagreements between economists exist within nations and cut across national boundaries. Since these disagreements tend to run along left-right lines, politicians are thrown back on their own political principles in seeking solutions for unemployment (cf. Rose, 1987a).

Functional interdependence can compel a common response by two or more different governments to deal with a problem effectively. Environmental pollution provides many examples of such problems. The wind carries airborne pollutants across city, state, and national boundaries. Hence, a local clean air act will be of no use if factories upwind of the city are emitting industrial pollutants. A state's clean water act will be of no effect if a river runs through several states, and sewage and other pollutants are dumped in the river upstream. A national government's antipollution programs will have limited effect if pollution is caused by emissions in another country, as is the case with acid rain that originates in the United States and affects Canada; pollution of the Rhine or the Danube as it wends through different European countries; or pollution of the Mediterranean by different national governments or by ships from other continents using the Mediterranean as a transit waterway (see, e.g., Hoberg, 1991; P. Haas, 1990).

When a problem arises from functional interdependence of

programs adopted by two or more governments, then different state or national governments must not only agree in recognizing a common problem but also agree about actions. For example, Canada's acid rain problem cannot be dealt with solely by Ottawa, for much of it is caused by prevailing winds exporting airborne American pollutants to Canada. A program to reduce acid rain in Canada thus requires legislation by the United States Congress as well as by the Canadian Parliament. Measures to clean up the Mediterranean require action by more than a dozen different countries that have jurisdiction over its shores. Interdependence creates a demand for the strongest form of lesson-drawing, namely, the adoption of a common policy by different governments, if the actions that any one government takes are to be effective in response to a collective problem.

Proceeding to Learn

Programs are designed rather than given by nature, and design is an art as well as a science, requiring judgment and skill. As Herbert Simon (1969: 54) has remarked: "Design is the core of all professional training; it is the principal mark that distinguishes the professions from the sciences." The professions include policy analysis and public finance, as well as medicine and the law. Professionals develop skills in designing policies through formal education and by learning from experience on the job (Bobrow and Dryzek, 1987). Professionals demonstrate their skills by diagnosing specific problems in the light of general principles and by making recommendations for action rather than by concentrating on explanation, the normal approach in the academic study of comparative politics.

Lesson-drawing is both a normative and a practical activity. It is normative insofar as a prescription that a program in effect elsewhere should be applied here is a statement about what ought to be done. But lesson-drawing is practical, too, for it is concerned with whether or not the prescription can be put into effect. Lesson-drawing thus differs from purely normative prescriptions that say nothing about how a prescribed goal can be achieved (cf. Majone, 1989: 40f).

LESSONS AS TOOLS

The procedures used to draw a lesson, like the lesson itself, are only means to political ends. The search for lessons is driven by a desire to find a program that will deal with a pressing political problem. Hence, we should think not only about how to learn, but even more about what is learned.

Tools are made to be applied; hence, lesson-drawing acts on Simon's (1979: 494) dictum that the real world is the most fertile of all sources of good ideas. The tradition of studying worldly experience in order to learn how to improve public policy was a practice that appealed to many of the founding fathers of social science. Alexis de Tocqueville (1954, 1: 14) examined democracy in America because, as he explained to his French readers, "My wish has been to find there instruction by which we may ourselves profit."

Unfortunately, many branches of the social sciences today carry abstraction to such a point that theories become non-applicable. Statistical evaluations routinely omit influences that are not readily quantified, even if they are important. To lend verisimilitude to unrealistic models, economists may enlarge their rhetoric to include "stylized facts" or even tell stories, that is, fables.

Today, most theoretical writing in the social sciences is not applicable, for an intellectual solution is not a practical solution if it is deduced from a theory that assumes away the actual causes of a problem. By contrast, in the physical sciences, even though theories may be stated in very abstract language, engineering sciences can apply basic principles of physics to the design of engineering products such as cameras, airplanes, and fax machines. If social science is to become a science like physics, then it, too, should be applicable to problems in the real world.

Lesson-drawing requires concepts, which come before theories. As a Nobel laureate in physics, Sir George Thompson (1961: 4) has emphasized: "Science depends on its concepts. These are the ideas which receive names. They determine the questions one asks, and the answers one gets. They are more fundamental than the theories which are stated in terms of them." Concepts provide common points of reference for grouping activities of agencies in different cities, states, or countries (Rose, 1991a). In an era in which quantitative methods have gained increasing esteem, it is well to remember that words—that is, concepts—are first of all needed to define the meaning of variables subject to quantitative analysis. The stipulation of concepts, particularly in the diagnosis of what the problem is for which a solution is sought, should guide the collection of quantifiable data. As Giovanni Sartori (1984: 10) emphasizes, "The better the concepts, the better the variables that can be derived from them." In the absence of concepts, numerical data is literally meaningless. If the words used to describe programs in different places are incommensurable or, in the case of foreign comparisons, untranslated, at best the result will be a series of case studies, but a collection of such stories is not a tool for action. Familiarity with the conceptual vocabulary of social science is a necessary precondition of lesson-drawing.

Familiarity with the logic of cause-and-effect models is also needed. A lesson is not a disjointed set of ideas about what to do. It requires a cause-and-effect model showing how a program designed on the basis of experience elsewhere can achieve a desired goal if adopted in the advocate's own jurisdiction.

The uncertainties of policy analysis have much more in common with medical diagnosis than with a mechanically predictable science (see Etzioni, 1985; McCloskey, 1984: 97f). Applying medical knowledge to individual patients is an art as well as a science. Success is more or less probable, not certain. The liability insurance that doctors carry is a reminder that medical prescriptions can have unanticipated effects.

The first task in policymaking, as in medicine, is to diagnose the cause of a complaint through disciplined inquiry. This is not always easy, for symptoms of disturbance can sometimes have multiple causes. Nevertheless, an accurate diagnosis is a precondition of designing a program that will have a reasonable probability of effectiveness. But when a doctor makes a prescription, he or she rarely guarantees success; the intention is to have a better than random chance of removing the causes of a complaint. Much the same is true of the programs that are prescribed as the result of lesson-drawing.

CONTINGENCY OF LESSONS

There is no certainty that a search of experience elsewhere will provide lessons that can lead to the design of a program that can be applied at home. The transfer of a program is affected by its specific context as well as by generic attributes.

Policymakers are accustomed to being forced to act under conditions of uncertainty when the consequences of a decision are disputed. Whatever the problem at hand, it is always possible to argue that a proposed program will not be effective, that is, realize the intentions of its sponsors. This is true whether the program is based on past experience within an organization, a speculative idea, or a lesson drawn from elsewhere. A distinctive feature of lesson-drawing is that one can always counter doubts with the argument, "The program works there."

A multiplicity of factors influence the outcome of the lesson-drawing process (see chapter 6). Power is a primary condition of applying a lesson in government. In Washington, a new program invariably requires a coalition of legislative and executive branch officials to take effect. Case studies of the policymaking process invariably emphasize the contingency of success (see, e.g., Kingdon, 1984). In a parliamentary system, power is centralized in a single governing party; coalition-building takes place within the executive branch.

Knowledge is a source of influencing those with power. Specialist knowledge of a repertoire of programs in effect elsewhere can gain an expert the ear of a policymaker wanting to do something. When policymakers are under great pressure to act and do not know what to do, policy entrepreneurs can market their prescriptions for action. If a prescription is accompanied by evidence that a similar measure has brought satisfaction elsewhere, then promoters of a new program gain greater credibility.

Resources are a second precondition for applying a lesson. If a proposed program calls for money or public personnel beyond the scope of a public agency, it cannot be introduced. Differences in resources are vast between local governments, for small towns and rural counties usually lack both the money and skilled personnel to implement major programs of large cities. The disparities in size between American states is substantial, but even the smallest state has hundreds of thousands of residents and a tax base that runs into the hundreds of millions or billions of dollars. At the international level, advanced industrial nations and Third World countries differ greatly, but OECD nations have relatively high levels of gross domestic product per capita. In this group of countries, military programs are most immediately affected by differences in size.

Expert opinion about what is technically possible is a third influence on lesson-drawing. Politicians responsible for making the final choice between program options often lack sufficient detailed knowledge to assess whether or not a lesson is likely to achieve its intended effects. If there is a positive consensus among experts about how a program will operate, this will reassure a policymaker who approves its goals. A consensus that a program will fail is a strong incentive to reject a proposal. Often experts disagree with each other about the effects of a lesson drawn from experience elsewhere. In such circumstances, policymakers make a choice between conflicting expert opinions as well as between conflicting program options.

The political values of policymakers are a fourth influence on the process of lesson-drawing from beginning to end. Decisions about whether a problem exists and the diagnosis of its causes reflect evaluations of what is satisfactory or unsatisfactory. Choices about where to search for solutions reflect ideological as well as cognitive biases. Choices about which lessons are politically possible and which should be ignored as politically impossible reflect values about what "must" be done and what is "not on" politically. The design of a program in the light of lessons elsewhere must take into account values as well as technical knowledge. Failure to take into account the values of the dominant coalition in government will leave a lesson in limbo; it can be applicable but, if politically unacceptable, it will not be applied.

ONE STEP AT A TIME

Even if policymaking often appears a process of pandemonium, a guide to lesson-drawing cannot be similarly confused. Before one can see how different activities occur simultaneously in the political process, one must first be able to recognize the elements that create the collective picture.

Defining terms is the first step in determining under what circumstances and to what extent programs in effect in one place can be transferred elsewhere. Chapter 2 defines what a lesson is; it also makes clear what a lesson is not. The basic steps in drawing a lesson are outlined, from scanning what is done elsewhere through the artful design of a program that is more likely to be an adaptation or a hybrid than a literal copy. The chapter also considers alternative answers to two interrelated questions: Is lesson-drawing possible? Who should decide if a lesson is desirable?

Searching for lessons is not the dominant activity of policymakers. Most of the time most programs run by routine. Chapter 3 considers the stimuli that force policymakers, whether elected officials or career civil servants, to depart from routine. The strongest impetus comes from dissatisfaction with the status quo. In searching for ideas about what to do to restore satisfaction, policymakers can turn to informal communities of experts, or to the experience of other public agencies within the same county or state within the same country, or to other countries or international organizations encouraging the diffusion of "best practice" programs across oceans. The search for lessons not only informs policymakers about what their counterparts elsewhere do, but also provides evidence to evaluate how well they themselves are doing by comparison with others.

Lesson-drawing leads to a search across both time and space. When drawing lessons across time, it is natural for policymakers to look to their own past. Chapter 4 shows that learning from the past is easier said than done. The records of the past are not organized to lead to prescriptions for action, and historians focus on understanding what happened, not prescribing for the present. Politicians are much more interested in the present and future than in what their predecessors did in office. The past may be abused as well as used, as in the casual drawing of analogies with the past in support of present interests and inclinations. If there is a measure that has brought satisfaction before—spending more money on an established program or invoking a standard response to a cyclical problem—it may suffice. But when what worked before no longer produces satisfaction, policymakers may speculate about the future, cautiously anticipating obstacles to the implementation of a new program or ambitiously deducing programs logically from theories. Since speculation is unbounded by empirical evidence from other times or places, it offers politicians the opportunity of substituting faith and will for reason and evidence.

Drawing lessons across space puts bounds on speculation, for attention is directed at programs already in effect, albeit somewhere else. This makes it easier to identify what is necessary to make a program operational. We would expect policymakers to look first at programs near at hand, but chapter 5 emphasizes that the definition of proximity is variable, not constant. In local government it can mean looking at the next county; for a governor, it is likely to mean looking at a nearby state. But for national policymakers, other countries are often the logical place to look. The choice of where to search also reflects subjective political values; governments that are nearest are not always most congenial, and distance may lend enchantment. This is particularly true when poor cities or states or nations want to "catch up" with those they perceive as most successful, such as postcommunist Eastern European nations seeking to catch up with West European neighbors. Techniques of lesson-drawing bridge distances of time and space through a prospective evaluation of the consequences of adopting here in the future a program already in effect there.

Whether a program can transfer from one place to another depends on seven conditions set out as hypotheses in chapter 6. Three of the hypotheses concern preconditions that are usually met within the United States or among a cluster of advanced industrial nations. The program in question should not concern a unique problem, suitable institutions should be available to deliver it, and sufficient resources of money, public personnel, and laws should be available. Four hypotheses concern much more variable contingencies. The simpler the cause-and-effect logic of a program, the more confident one can be about drawing a positive lesson; complex programs have more obstacles to transfer. Programs involving small-scale changes face fewer obstacles than those involving large-scale change. Interdependence between programs of different jurisdictions or different nations increases learning. Since politicians are concerned with the goals of public policy, it is not enough that a program transfer effectively; it must also be consistent with the values of policymakers.

Obstacles to lesson-drawing are not permanent; in the course of time many obstacles become variables. Chapter 7 emphasizes that changes in the policy environment—a downturn in the economy or the cumulative effects of demographic change—cause changes in the effects of a program. This can convert satisfaction into dissatisfaction. The likelihood of changes in each of the contingencies of lesson-drawing is then reviewed. Values that veto the adoption of a lesson in the short run are among the least stable obstacles to applying lessons in the long run, for the swing of the electoral pendulum can remove from office a party opposing a measure, and the threat of electoral defeat if action is not taken to remove dissatisfaction can lead to fresh openness to ideas. Distances between places change as time goes by. In the past generation the barriers between the American North and South have lowered, and the fall of the Berlin Wall has removed a great barrier to interchange between East and West. In the fullness of time, changes in society create demands for action, and obstacles to lesson-drawing can disappear.

To help readers understand the application of general principles to concrete problems, the significance of generic concepts is illustrated by reference to specific problems facing state and local governments, national governments, and the governments of advanced industrial nations on many continents. The examples are intended to help readers faced with diverse problems learn to become better and more self-conscious drawers of lessons from their own experience and the experience of others.

What Is Lesson-drawing?

A wise man's question is half the answer.

— Old proverb

When policymakers seek the resolution of a pressing problem, the starting point is a question: What to do? A search of one's own experience and what is done elsewhere is undertaken instrumentally, in hopes of finding an answer. But in order to draw a lesson, it is necessary to search analytically rather than anecdotally. The collection of stories about how others deal with their problems is insufficient. In order to draw a valid lesson, searchers must be more than mere travelers; they should understand the principles and practice of lesson-drawing.

Because policymakers have a large fund of experience on which to draw, methods of lesson-drawing or questions about the aptness of prescriptions are rarely raised. Policymakers tend to take for granted that they know what questions to ask and what experience is relevant when prescribing actions on the basis of unselfconscious lesson-drawing.

The International Monetary Fund (IMF) is an example of an organization staffed by expert economists who prescribe lessons for countries seeking to escape from the consequences of economic mismanagement (see, e.g., Tait, 1990). A senior IMF official illustrates how theoretical knowledge can lead to a practical conclusion when advising a particular Third World country: "I tell them that if their inflation rate is 150 percent and their interest rate is 100 percent, sooner or later they are going to face a big problem." Because IMF staff are continuously monitoring economic conditions in more than 150 countries, collectively it has a vast experience of monetary problems around the globe. This experience is frequently cited as validating the lessons that it offers countries in economic difficulty. In the words of the IMF's managing director, Michel Camdessus (1989: 369): "The experience of the IMF is, of course, very varied, based on its continuous contacts with governments. Through all these activities, the Fund has amassed a wealth of experience and a viewpoint about what policies work, and what policies do not work."

Many of the maxims that policymakers draw from their experience are not based on theory or logic, nor are they consistently supported by empirical tests, as would be the case with a hypothesis advanced in a scientific setting. Maxims uncritically drawn from experience can even be contradictory: "It is a fatal defect of the current principles of administration that, like proverbs, they occur in pairs. For almost every principle one can find an equally plausible and acceptable contradictory principle" (Simon 1947: 20). Even if maxims can be supported with many examples from a particular policy area or place, this does not make them universal truths valid across time and space.

The import and export of programs through lesson-drawing is valid only if systematic care is taken in analyzing under what circumstances and to what extent a program in effect in one place could be effective in another. The purpose of this chapter is to outline this process. The first section defines what a lesson is and differentiates lesson-drawing from other approaches to public policy. Four major steps in drawing a lesson—searching elsewhere, developing a model of how a program operates, creating a new program, and evaluating transfer prospectively—are described in the second section. Scholars give conflicting answers to the question: Is lesson-drawing possible? The third section explains why lesson-drawing is merely inevitable, since contemporary governments cannot exist in isolation. The concluding section asks, under what circumstances is lesson-drawing desirable?

Defining a Lesson

Lesson-drawing is concerned with whether programs are fungible, that is, capable of being put into effect in more than one place. Because lesson-drawing is only one part of the policy process, it is important to be clear not only about what it is but also about what it is not.

LESSONS AS A BASIS FOR ACTION

In the policy process a lesson can be defined as *a program for action based on a program or programs undertaken in another city, state, or nation, or by the same organization in its own past.* Lessons can be drawn across time, as in frequently invoked "lessons of history." An organization's own past is one fruitful source of experience, but lessons can also be drawn across space. The boundaries crossed depend on the involvement of policymakers with local, state, or national problems. Because policymakers are action-oriented, a lesson focuses on specific measures that a public agency can undertake; it is not concerned with the academic analysis of determinants of policy beyond the control of public officials.

A lesson is more complex than a simple maxim or a general decision rule. It takes the form of a *program* specifying the cause-and-effect mechanisms by which government actions are expected to produce a specific policy outcome. A program includes laws and regulations authorizing action, an administrative agency responsible for delivering it, an appropriation of money, public employees to deliver the service, and rules for determining which individuals or organizations receive the program's outputs (Rose, 1985a). Programs are designed; they belong to the world of artifice or synthesis.

Lessons are activities of *angewandte Sozialwissenschaft* (applied social science); the German phrase emphasizes that scientific methods can be used not only to explain social phenomena but also to influence them. Just as an engineer starts with the idea of a problem that is to be resolved and then designs something to reach that goal, so programs can be considered as instruments or tools to achieve policy objectives (Hood, 1986; Linder and Peters, 1989).

Transferability of a program is a distinguishing feature of lesson-drawing. The critical question is *whether* a program in one setting is capable of being put into effect in another. The bottom line in lesson-drawing is not the explanation of a measure's initial effect but an assessment of the consequences of putting something similar in effect elsewhere.

A lesson must allow for the fact that two places or two points in time in an agency's history are never exactly identical in every respect. A lesson is like a jazz number that is more or less based on the chords of a preexisting standard tune. In the process, there is both intentional selection and unintentional adaptation (cf. Westney, 1987: 24ff).

A lesson can conclude with a positive endorsement or be negative, warning of difficulties in imitating what is done elsewhere. It may also be conditional, stating: "If you want to do X, then program A is likely to achieve this goal." The American Freedom of Information Act is an example of a program that has been widely studied by foreign nations, yet different countries have drawn conflicting lessons (Bennett, 1991a). In Canada the act became a stimulus for the government to adopt a similar measure, given strong political support for open government. In Britain, where official secrecy is valued by policymakers, the act became a negative exemplar, cited as evidence of difficulties in such a program.

Lesson-drawing cannot be politically neutral, because politics is about conflicting values and goals. A lesson is always a means to a political end. Contrasting conclusions were drawn from examinations of the Freedom of Information Act because those approaching it did so with contrasting values. Whether a lesson is politically controversial depends on the extent to which there is a consensus about political values among those studying experience elsewhere and the fit between the program's normative assumptions and the values of those examining it. There is rarely complete consensus, even about seemingly scientific and technical matters such as promoting health and safety (see, e.g., Wildavsky, 1988).

The greater the political importance of an issue, the more likely there is to be controversy about both program means and policy ends. In economic policy, there are disputes about whether reducing inflation or reducing unemployment should have higher priority, and disputes about the particular program best able to reduce inflation or unemployment. The policy recommendations that the IMF draws from its experience are often criticized in countries receiving its lessons. When the controversy is about the goals of economic policy, then the more successful a prescribed lesson is, the more it will be attacked by those who reject its purpose. In a political controversy, lessons can be pitted against each other, with the lesson having the support of the strongest battalions carrying the day.

The functional concerns of policymakers are diverse. Only a small minority specialize in activities that concern many policy areas, such as budgeting or personnel administration. The great majority tend to specialize. This is even more true of career civil servants. Even if policymakers work for the same government or serve the same administration, when their policy responsibilities are very different, they are restricted in what they can learn from each other, because the programs for which they are responsible have little in common.

Functional divisions among the agencies of a city, state, or country create links between agencies facing similar problems in different government jurisdictions. Local officials are likely to be interested in what is done by counterparts with similar tasks in other cities, other states, and even in other countries. From the perspective of an education official, teaching mathematics presents the same issues whether one is in Massachusetts or California, or in North America, Europe, or Asia. Teachers must be trained to teach the subject, and children must learn how to do arithmetic and higher math.

WHAT LESSON-DRAWING IS NOT

Lesson-drawing is not a theory of how policymakers learn; that belongs to the world of social psychology (cf. Etheredge, 1981, 1985). It is about what is learned, the programs that public officials develop in efforts to deal with immediate substantive problems.

Lesson-drawing makes use of concepts and methods found in many fields of political science. But because the focus is on the transfer of programs, it is not the same as conventional comparison for its own sake; the study of the process of innovation and diffusion of policies; or the analysis of the role of ideas, institutions, analogies, or symbols in policymaking.

The comparative study of public policy is concerned with the way in which different governments respond to a common problem. Comparisons can be made in terms of programs (how big cities deal with urban decay); resources (how much money is spent on urban programs); or outcomes (urban crime rates). When quantitative measures are available, it is possible to produce a "league table," that is, a table that ranks states or countries from highest to lowest on a given measure.

The identification of differences in inputs or outputs invites explanation. A major concern of comparative social science is to test alternative theories offering explanations through after-the-fact analysis of observed differences in programs (see Dogan and Pelassy, 1990). The result is a set of statements explaining why a program that produced a given effect in country X did or did not do so in country Y, or why the existence of a common problem, such as rising unemployment, led to the adoption of one type of program in a given group of countries, and to another type in a second group.

Logically, the observation of differences could lead to hypotheses about whether a program now in effect in country X would be effective if transferred to country Y. The great majority of studies in comparative public policy avoid this. The object is to explain what has already happened. However, policymakers in country Y want to use knowledge about what happens elsewhere to improve their future, not to explain current shortcomings.

The study of innovation is different from lesson-drawing because innovation research is concerned with novel programs. Lesson-drawing, by contrast, presupposes that even though a program may be new to a government considering it, something very much like it will already be in effect elsewhere. Whereas an innovation is about something new, a lesson is a shortcut that relies on experience elsewhere as a source of knowledge. An agency that draws a lesson does not have to pay the price for being the first to try a novel idea; it can learn from the experience and the mistakes of others. Lesson-drawing is about the diffusion of what was once an innovation elsewhere.

Although there is a logical connection between lesson-drawing and diffusion studies, political scientists in this field have been surprisingly indifferent to the actual content of programs diffused. The issue is not whether a particular type of response has been made, but whether a state has done anything at all in a given field of policy. Programs adopted by different states in response to a common or similar problem are treated as if they were more or less identical. The focus is on general categories of policy concern, such as welfare, education, or civil rights (cf. Gray, 1973, and Eyestone, 1977: 443ff). Ignoring differences between programs prevents lesson-drawing, for it obscures what specifically each government does.

Diffusion studies are usually concerned with the timing and sequence of program adoption. The initial aim is to identify why some governments are leaders in a process of adoption and some are laggards (Walker, 1969; Collier and Messick, 1975; Savage, 1985; Berry and Berry, 1990). The second step is to explain why governments differ in their readiness to act. Diffusion may be explained by geographical propinquity, the availability of resources, or the attributes of government. The emphasis is on sequence: "The major problem of this research tradition is that it reveals nothing about the content of new policies. Its fascination is with process, not substance" (Clark, 1985: 63).

Diffusion studies are often technocratic, assuming that there is a political consensus about political ends, and thus about program means. Efficiency and effectiveness are assumed to be common values pervasive among policymakers. Hence, programs to treat a disease with a new drug or to use a new seed to grow more profitable farm crops are evaluated as more or less efficient (cf. Rogers, 1983). In politics, however, conflicts about goals are pervasive. For example, the high-tax, high-welfare programs of California and New York are unlikely to appeal to southern states where low welfare benefits and taxes are regarded as desirable.

Lessons differ from the big ideas that cause a paradigm shift in the way in which policymakers perceive the world, such as the Keynesian revolution in economic policy or the green revolution in thinking about the environment (cf. Kuhn, 1962). A paradigm shift involves a major intellectual reorientation that has a pervasive effect on the way in which many problems and programs are viewed; by contrast, a lesson is directed at one particular problem and program. By definition, a paradigm shift is an abnormal interruption in the policymaking process. Lesson-drawing is about the everyday activities of policymakers working within an established paradigm. Because conflict often occurs between new and old paradigms, as in the reception in economics of Keynesian theory, the intellectual rationale of a new program does not provide unchallenged lessons for public policy (cf. Hall, 1989).

The analysis of institutions is traditionally central in the study of government, but it is not to be confused with lesson-drawing. Much writing about institutions is purely descriptive of procedures without regard to the programs that are their outputs. It is a truism to say that every public program requires some kind of institutional basis, but this does not offer any particular guidance to policymakers. Even if after-the-fact analysis can demonstrate that institutions do affect programs, the literature of public administration is ambiguous or inadequate in offering prescriptions about which types of institutions ought to be adopted to achieve specific program goals (cf. March and Olsen, 1989; Hood and Jackson, 1991). Lesson-drawing and institutional analysis become one only when proponents of political change argue that institutions in effect elsewhere, for example, the proportional representation method of election, should be adopted here.

Lessons differ from the analogies that constitute the "lessons" of history. Analogies depend on identifying one or a few similarities between past and present that are assumed to be so powerful that they override all other differences. Policymakers with superficial knowledge of the past and no concern with historical accuracy can thus invoke analogies with abandon. The authors of *Thinking in Time* conclude that most contemporary American policymakers know so little history that instead of trying to distill lessons from the past, they use past events "for advocacy or for comfort" (Neustadt and May, 1986: xii). Lesson-drawing seeks to identify rather than ignore obstacles to generalizing from the past to the present.

Invoking the name of another city, state, or foreign country as an argument in favor of or against a program is not lesson-drawing; rather, it is the manipulation of a symbol of success or failure. In the rhetoric of politics, symbols can be used to place an idea on the political agenda. In the United States today, Japan is often invoked as an emotionally charged symbol; Sweden and Britain are other countries that may be evoked as symbols of something to emulate or to avoid (cf. Edelman, 1964; Robertson, 1991). The protean character of symbols makes them useful in political controversy, but because symbols are vague and ambiguous, their use has little to do with drawing lessons about the effectiveness of specific programs.

A lesson is much more than a symbol invoked to sway opinion about a policy and more than a dependent variable telling a social scientist what is to be explained. A lesson is a detailed cause-and-effect description of a set of actions that government can consider in the light of experience elsewhere, including a prospective evaluation of whether what is done elsewhere could someday become effective here.

Drawing a Lesson

The practical problem of lesson-drawing is not whether to select information, but how. The process of drawing a lesson involves four analytically distinct stages. The first is searching experience for programs that, in another place or time, appear to have brought satisfaction. Second, it is necessary to abstract a cause-and-effect model from what is observed. The third stage is to create a lesson, that is, a new program for action based on what has been learned elsewhere. Finally, a prospective evaluation is needed to estimate the consequences of adopting the lesson, drawing on empirical evidence from elsewhere, and speculating about what will happen in the future if the lesson is applied.

SEARCHING EXPERIENCE

The first step in drawing a lesson is to search for information about programs that have been introduced elsewhere to deal with a problem similar to that confronting the searchers. As subsequent chapters demonstrate, the potential scope for search is vast, yet the starting point is not random.

Searching can extend across time or space, depending on the problem at hand. In budgeting, officials normally search the past, comparing expenditures from previous years with this year's expenditures and proposals for next year's expenditures (Wildavsky, 1988a: chapter 3). Capital expenditures on major projects such as roads and bridges can lead to "searching" the future for an estimate of the use that is likely to be made of a proposed highway or bridge after it is built.

Searching across space is influenced by the level of government at which a problem arises. Local officials tend to turn to parallel agencies in other cities or counties; state officials to other state capitals; and national policymakers, in addition to examining their own past, may look to counterparts in foreign countries. In an international system that is becoming increasingly open, ideas can flow across national boundaries as well as across state and local boundaries.

The object of the search is to find a program that "works." From a narrowly technical point of view, we can say that a program works if it has been implemented and remains in effect. A program that works differs from a program that cannot be implemented, just as an effective mechanical appliance differs from one that is unreliable or cannot be made to operate. A technical judgment that a program is effective should not be confused with a political judgment. From a political perspective, a program works if it produces more satisfaction than dissatisfaction within the government responsible for it.

Experience is not examined to produce history for its own sake or a treatise in comparative public policy, but to gain fresh insight into one's own problems here and now. Policymakers need "funded experience" (Nailor, 1991: 25), knowledge that is sufficiently general to be capable of being transferred to the searcher's own agency, yet sufficiently specific to be applicable to a particular problem.

MAKING A MODEL

The second step is analytic: creating a conceptual model of how programs deal with a specific problem. A model should not describe a program's attributes using words that are nation-specific. A model should be generic, specifying the basic elements in clear concepts. Since lesson-drawing is about transferring measures from one place to another, it is counterproductive for a model to resemble a full-scale historical study or to be a journalistic description that concentrates on named individuals and events. Such ideographic details confuse what is specific to time and place with what is generic, and thus portable.

A model is more than a taxonomy or checklist of program requirements. It also specifies cause-and-effect relationships that make a program operate effectively. Working models are familiar in engineering; for example, a model of an automobile engine shows how an internal combustion engine operates. Such an engineering model is not designed as an exact replica of a particular manufacturer's engine for a particular car in a particular year. It is a generic model demonstrating basic principles of a car engine. The inability or incapacity to produce a model showing how a program will operate is a sign that policymakers rely less on analysis than on faith.

A cause-and-effect model specifies procedures for delivering a service, the actions that must be taken inside the "black box" of government to turn a policy intention into an identifiable program. A model thus differs from a summary statistic such as a cost-benefit ratio, which reduces the complexities of delivering a program to a single number. Detailing the mechanics of a program is particularly important in lesson-drawing based on foreign experience. It guards against selective perceptions that highlight the easy or attractive parts of a program and leave in shadow the hard parts needed to make it effective (Muniak, 1985).

CREATING A LESSON

Knowledge gained from experience elsewhere is the starting point in designing a program for adoption here. An element of creativity is required, for differences in time and space normally make impossible a carbon copy of a program in effect elsewhere.

Because a model is a construct instead of a photographic description, the elements that constitute it can readily be modified —provided that the removal of an element is matched by its replacement by a functional equivalent and that additions are not counterproductive. Flexibility is needed to take into account differences in circumstances between the agency "exporting" an idea and the agency considering its import.

The simplest way to draw a lesson is to *copy* a program (table 2.1). Within a nation, copying is often possible, because of the identity or close similarity of institutions and laws. Since 1892 the National Conference of Commissioners on Uniform State Laws has been drafting model legislation on matters as diverse as alcoholism treatment, foreign money claims, and conservation of historic buildings. It has had significant success in promoting the enactment of more than one hundred model laws in dozens of states (Council of State Governments, 1990: 405ff). Copying is more difficult across national boundaries. Even if national governments are analytically no more than intervening variables, policymakers cannot ignore the variations due to differences in language and in legal procedures.

TABLE 2.1
ALTERNATIVE WAYS OF DRAWING A LESSON

1. COPYING	Enacting more or less intact a program already in effect in another jurisdiction.
2. ADAPTATION	Adjusting for contextual differences a program already in effect in another jurisdiction.
3. MAKING A HYBRID	Combining elements of programs from two different places.
4. SYNTHESIS	Combining familiar elements from programs in a number of different places to create a new program.
5. INSPIRATION	Using programs elsewhere as an intellectual stimulus to develop a novel program.

Adaptation occurs when a program in effect elsewhere is the starting point for the design of a new program allowing for differences in institutions, culture, and historical specifics. Adaptation rejects copying every detail of a program; instead, it uses a particular measure as a guide to what can be done (see, e.g., Waltman, 1980). Adaptation involves two governments in a one-to-one relationship of pacesetter and follower. Japan's late nineteenth-century adaptation of programs from the United States and European countries is a textbook example of this relationship.

A *hybrid* combines recognizable elements from programs in two different places. If, for example, policymakers in a federal system want to transfer a program that is in use in a unitary system, the substance may be borrowed from one country and the administrative delivery system from their own system. In whatever way the different elements are combined, each of the principal parts of a hybrid program can be observed in action, albeit in different places.

A *synthesis* combines elements familiar in different programs into a distinctive and fresh whole. The logic is comparable to assembling familiar parts of human anatomy to produce a unique human figure. For example, every democratic country can claim that its electoral system is a unique combination of laws and administrative procedures concerning voter registration, electoral districting, ballot forms, election day procedures, and converting votes into seats in the national legislature (cf. Mackie and Rose, 1991: 509ff). Yet governments challenged to write a new election law, as happened in Eastern Europe following the collapse of one-party communist systems, do not seek to invent new election procedures unknown elsewhere. Instead, each government has produced a synthesis of familiar elements combined in ways suited to its national circumstances (White, 1990).

The examination of programs elsewhere can be a source of *inspiration* instead of analysis. When a policymaker unaccustomed to travel views a familiar problem in an unfamiliar setting, this can inspire fresh ideas about what might be done at home. However, enthusiasm does not produce a detailed model of a program in effect elsewhere. It may even encourage the enthusiast to overlook faults or critical elements that are difficult to adapt. Inspiration can produce a proposal that is a breath of fresh air. However, this also connotes an unsubstantial foundation. Because experience elsewhere cannot be used to evaluate an inspired program, it is less a form of lesson-drawing than of speculation.

Taxation is a field in which copying, adaptation, hybridization, and synthesis frequently operate. There are more than 150 different nations in the world, but there are not 150 completely different ways in which to levy a sales tax or an income tax. International institutions such as the International Monetary Fund and the Organization for Economic Cooperation and Development (OECD) have experts who can draw upon their theoretical knowledge and practical experience about different types of taxes, the preconditions that must be met to introduce a given type of tax, and the variations that can be introduced in its application (see, e.g., Goode, 1984; Tanzi, 1987). Although the particulars of a tax may vary, the alternatives for choice are limited. For example, a value-added tax (VAT) is now in effect in forty-six countries scattered across every continent. A government considering the adoption of VAT can draw on this experience in designing its own value-added tax (Tait, 1988).

PROSPECTIVE EVALUATION ACROSS
TIME AND SPACE

Because the applicability of a lesson is contingent, the final stage in lesson-drawing is a prospective evaluation of the likelihood that a proposed program would be effective. An analysis across time and space is both comparative and dynamic. Where state or nation X is today, we hope to be tomorrow; their present is meant to become our future.

Whereas the past is given, the future is not. The starting point is what is known now—the way in which a program operates elsewhere. Prospective evaluation combines empirical evidence about how a program operates in place X with hypotheses about the likely future effects of a similar program in place Y. While any statement about the future inevitably has an element of speculation, prospective evaluation is bounded by empirical observation of a program already in effect; speculation is limited to reckoning future consequences of introducing something similar elsewhere. Although the conclusions of prospective evaluation are not certain, comparison of existing programs with a proposed program provides more empirical evidence than does a prospective evaluation based solely on assumptions about the future.

Prospective evaluation differs from conventional evaluation research, because the latter is retrospective, examining a program after it has been in effect for several years. In conventional evaluation research, familiar social science methods can be used to observe behavior, collect data, and undertake statistical tests. Because evaluations of public programs often take place in a highly charged political context, evaluators may be subject to constraints. Even when evaluators are free to proceed as they wish, conclusions are rarely conclusive, because strictly controlled experiments cannot be undertaken as in a laboratory (cf. Weiss, 1972).

Conventional evaluation research produces too much information too late. Because retrospective evaluation relies on evidence only available after a program has been in effect for several years, policymakers under pressure to act cannot use it. The demand of policymakers is not for after-the-fact evaluation but for before-the-fact assessments that indicate whether the most effective course of action is to copy program A, adapt program B, go for a hybrid or synthesis of a number of programs, or make an inspired leap into the unknown.

Prospective evaluation starts by observing how a program operates in another country and developing a model of what is required for it to produce its effects there. A review of experience elsewhere in introducing similar programs provides lessons about problems of implementation (cf. Pressman and Wildavsky, 1974: 143).

Prospective evaluation is concerned not only with whether a program can be implemented but also with what substantive effects it may have. It is routinely used in tax policy. The future effects of a proposed tax can be calculated by relating the tax rates to the tax base specified in the program. This requires estimating the value of the tax base after a law is enacted and the effectiveness of tax administration. Each year the budget process starts with a forecast, based on past experience and anticipated changes in the economy, of the revenue yield of existing tax legislation. As proposals for changing tax laws are considered, each is evaluated in terms of its impact on revenue; a 1 percent change in a tax rate may appear small, but it can alter revenue by millions, hundred of millions, or billions of dollars.

If a new tax is under consideration, then it is virtually certain that it will already be in effect somewhere else. If it is totally novel, this constitutes a caution for policymakers anxious to avoid the risks of experimentation. Within the United States, there is substantial variability in forms of taxes; some cities and states have income tax, sales tax, or tax exemptions to attract industry; others do not. Hence, jurisdictions contemplating adopting a tax already in effect elsewhere can examine its operations in order to draw lessons about designing a measure and to aid in the prospective evaluation of its likely effects.

The purpose of prospective evaluation is forewarning as well as foreknowledge. Whereas retrospective evaluation documents actions that are not easily undone, prospective evaluation gives warning of what to avoid, and it can do so early enough for this to be taken into account when drawing a lesson. Forewarning can lead to the better design of a new program, or to the conclusion that a program that works elsewhere cannot work here.

Is Lesson-drawing Possible?

Technical feasibility is taken for granted in abstract theories of social science. Programs are assumed to be perfectly fungible, applicable anywhere and everywhere. The logic is that of an engineering science, which starts with a model of how an automobile works. It is then engineered so it can be manufactured and operate anywhere, and parts can be exchanged between Fords made in Detroit, Cologne, and Barcelona.

At the other extreme, theories grounded in history, institutions, and culture assume total blockage, the impossibility of transferring a program from one country to another or from one city to another or even of applying past experience to the present. Each problem is regarded as having a unique configuration of characteristics specific to a particular time and place. In such theories, the most important feature of an American or British or German tax is not any generic attribute of taxation discussed in economics textbooks but whether it is enacted by the United States Congress, the British Parliament, or the German *Bundestag*.

The ideas of perfect fungibility and total blockage are logically contradictory. The former assumes that lesson-drawing is always possible, and the latter that it is invariably impossible. In the real world we do not expect anything to be perfectly fungible or totally blocked. The critical questions concern the extent to which fungibility or isolation is possible. Understanding the assumptions of each ideal-type argument is helpful in identifying conditions that can make it more or less possible to transfer programs across space and time.

TOTAL FUNGIBILITY

The starting point is the existence of common problems, defined in terms sufficiently abstract so that generic solutions appear applicable everywhere. Differences between cities, countries, or continents are dismissed as of no consequence. Even if experts disagree about what should be done, they share the assumption that there are a very limited number of programs that can respond to a problem, and that a program should work much the same wherever adopted. Thus, Steve H. Hanke, a university-based economist who consults in many countries and continents as well as in Washington, explains: "I tell everyone the same thing" (Libowitz, 1991: 49).

Economic theory assumes fungibility. Policy instruments are designed to work within a stylized one-dimensional model of an economic system that achieves clarity by omitting political and institutional phenomena. Policy prescriptions are treated as universally valid, for the system described in the model is expected to work the same irrespective of time and place. Lawrence Summers (1991: 2), chief economist of the World Bank, can start a talk on "Lessons of Reform" by emphasizing:

First, *respect the universal laws of economics.* There is a strong tendency in badly performing economies with demanding populations to suppose that there are special principles that apply locally, or that some new type of economic system can work miracles. Action on these beliefs is usually a prelude to disaster.

Political necessity does not suspend economic laws. There are no viable alternatives for reforming economies to the necessary actions—stabilization, privatization and liberalization. (Italics in the original.)

The world of consumer goods provides many familiar examples of total fungibility. IBM PCs, Sony Walkmen, and Mercedes cars and trucks sell worldwide; they are the same products, notwithstanding differences in the cultures and institutions of their customers. The globalization of McDonalds is particularly striking, for even though the need for food is universal, nothing would seem more American and culture-specific than fast-food hamburgers. Yet McDonalds sells hamburgers not only all over America but also in Hamburg, the German city that gave the food its name, in Moscow, and in Tokyo.

The public policy equivalent of franchising is the capacity to pluralize programs, reproducing standard service-delivery units in many places. A fire department's stations are much the same throughout a city. Although every state has many school districts, the design of schools takes a limited number of easily reproduced forms. Pluralization accounts for much of the growth of government. By replicating programs as a retail chain increases its number of outlets, American federal, state, and local government has expanded to provide services to a population that has grown by more than 100 million people in the postwar era (see Kochen and Deutsch, 1980: 33f; Rose, 1985b, 1988b: 116ff).

Insofar as advanced industrial societies are converging in their social and economic conditions, it should be increasingly possible for programs to transfer from one country to another. Within a nation, convergence can be facilitated by the interregional movement of population and the diffusion of common ideas through the mass media. Internationally, there is a substantial movement of people and ideas, and this is particularly so in Europe, where distances are short by American standards and national boundaries are increasingly permeable (cf. Kerr, 1983; Studlar, 1987; Bennett, 1991b).

Differences in economic achievements among advanced industrial societies raise questions about total fungibility. Inflation and unemployment have been problems in every advanced industrial nation in the past two decades, and there is an international "market" in programs to reduce unemployment and to fight inflation. Yet after an international search for programs to combat inflation and unemployment, Bruno and Sachs (1985: 274) conclude:

> It would seem only natural that a theory for a country's or several countries' response can only be formulated if one takes its specific institutional or structural features into consideration. However, macro-theory, whether Keynesian or monetarist, has for a long time tended to consider one and the same basic model as applicable to all economies.

Adherence to abstraction for its own sake results in lessons drawn from abstract economic theories facing difficulties in application to any one real country. This is a step backward from lesson-drawing, which generalizes from actual experience to a prospective evaluation of effects in a second country. Nobel laureate Robert Solow (1985: 329) recommends that economists reduce the risk of irrelevance by becoming more realistic in assumptions, developing "a collection of models contingent on society's circumstances—on the historical context, you might say—and not a single monolithic model for all seasons."

Fungibility presupposes political agreement about goals. It is possible for educators to look to other states or countries for programs that appear effective in teaching children arithmetic, for there is agreement that this is desirable. Differences in government at the national level, whether constitutional (e.g., a presidential or parliamentary system), partisan (a right, center, or left government), or organizational (a devolved or centralized delivery system) are not immediately relevant in teaching arithmetic in the classroom. The presumption is that a program to teach arithmetic can be effective in many different societies.

However, few policy areas are free of all dispute about policy goals or the institutions that deliver programs. In the United States, there are recurring political disputes about what ought to be the priorities of schools. In every country there are value conflicts among economists about what government ought to do, and differences among nations in the institutions of economic policymaking. Even though academic social scientists may ignore such "details," policymakers cannot.

TOTAL BLOCKAGE

Lesson-drawing is deemed impossible in theories assuming that every country, or even every state or city, is a unique configuration of culture, institutions, and history. Blockage occurs when factors specific to place and time are of overwhelming importance, resulting in every program being designed to fit a unique configuration of circumstances. Insofar as this is the case, the transfer of programs based on experience elsewhere is impossible.

More than two millennia ago, Heraclitus argued that one cannot step into the same river twice. Even if the banks and the riverbed are the same, the water that flows through is different. Whatever the similarities between past and present, the configuration of circumstances is never identical. Similarly, however small the distance between two places on the map and however similar the social, economic, and political composition of their populations, by definition they cannot be the same.

Stressing the uniqueness of different points in time leads to the extreme implication that an organization cannot rely on its past experience when facing present difficulties. The speed of contemporary change adds relevance to the idea that contemporary policymakers can no longer learn from their own past, for: "The past is a foreign country; they do things differently there" (Hartley, 1953: 1).

An alternative view is that the past and present are inextricably linked; a newly elected government inherits the responsibility of carrying out all the programs that its predecessors have enacted. At any given moment in time, the majority of programs administered by the government of the day are not of its own choice but inherited from administrations that left office decades or even generations ago. The precedence of inheritance before choice blocks lesson-drawing insofar as it is not possible to alter programs already in place (cf. Rose and Davies, forthcoming).

When historians describe important determinants of programs in terms unique to each country, they endorse the view that nation-specific determinants of a program are critical, even though similar programs, for example, social security, are adopted in different countries in response to common stimuli. The determinants of past decisions become obstacles to lesson-drawing insofar as the result is to make a program path dependent; that is, "the consequence of small events and chance circumstances" not only determines the specific content of a program but also "locks in" commitments to a course of action that current policymakers may regard as inferior to practices elsewhere, yet are unable to change (Arthur, 1988: 11).

The values and beliefs of a political culture can also block the transfer of a program (cf. King, 1973; Lipset, 1990). These determine what is or is not acceptable politically; they also create symbolic attachments that cannot be easily abandoned. For example, Americans do not consider proportional representation as more effective in achieving the goal of one person, one vote, one value; the first-past-the-post electoral system is regarded as part of "the American way." Differences in culture are sometimes described as contrasts in national "styles" of government. Insofar as styles differ, a program in effect elsewhere may be blocked from transferring if it is out of harmony with the style of a government considering it (cf. Richardson, 1982; Freeman, 1985: 481ff). Even though cultural norms may not be perfectly fixed (Eckstein, 1992: chapter 7), in the short period that politicians have in office, they must be taken as given.

American race relations illustrates how historical differences created obstacles to transferring programs from one part of the United States to another or between countries. The southern states have been unique among advanced industrial nations in a heritage of slavery and legal segregation. Hence, when the civil rights crisis arose in America in the 1960s, unprecedented measures were required to treat the unique circumstances of the Deep South. No lessons could be drawn from northern states, because they lacked the same history. Small-scale immigration to European societies has faced governments there with problems of multiracial societies. However, differences in race relations history mean that European governments rarely draw on the United States for lessons.

Theories of total blockage justify analysis of policymaking in terms of specific details about the personalities and conflicting interests of policymakers, and journalists give blow-by-blow accounts of the adoption of a new program. Even though details may have little theoretical significance, they are treated as crucial in determining what governments do and do not do.

A critical assumption of blockage is that each country, state, or city is a *gestalt*, a whole with qualities different from the sum of its parts. Gestaltists accept that even though similarities exist between programs and governments, they are unimportant by contrast with the unique configuration of attributes within each society. The distinctiveness of this configuration blocks the transfer of programs, despite the many similarities between parts.

The argument for total blockage is overdetermined. To suggest that any one part of a society can determine the whole goes far beyond the commonplace description of a society as a seamless web. It asserts that anything can determine everything else. Yet there is no substantial reason to believe, for example, that whether a country has a presidential or a parliamentary system of government will determine the programs it uses for paying unemployment benefits or providing parks and recreation. To assert that history imposes a permanent block on drawing lessons ignores the significance of the passage of time. Just as the present constrains past choices, in the fullness of time present actions can alter the future (Rose and Davies, forthcoming: chapter 2).

IS ISOLATION POSSIBLE?

The idea that any nation's government can live in isolation from the rest of the world is a caricature. In state and local policymaking, intergovernmental relations are an integral part of everyday activities. Every national government has diplomats, defense officials, trade officials, and central bankers who spend their time pondering the impact of what happens in other nations on events at home. Even the most isolationist of communist powers, Albania, could maintain its uniquely introverted system for only a year after the fall of the Iron Curtain in Europe.

Setting out the requirements of total isolation can illustrate the impossibility of policymakers totally ignoring what happens elsewhere. In local government, this could occur only in a fortified city-state in a remote mountainous area of no interest to other governments, armies, or marauding bands. Such isolation was difficult to maintain in the Middle Ages; it is impossible in OECD nations today. The United States abandoned its traditional policy of diplomatic and military isolation a half-century ago. In Europe countries such as Sweden and Switzerland have been neutral but not isolated; keeping out of war has required an active awareness of what their larger neighbors are doing. In the 1990s, the revolution in communications, moving information across boundaries by telephone, fax, communications satellites, and jet plane, means that a government must be without telephone lines or roads to achieve total isolation. If a country were like that, it would not be a modern society.

Because programs are the unit of analysis in lesson-drawing, generalizations about total fungibility and total blockage have little meaning. The object of lesson-drawing is not to make Mississippians like Minnesotans, Poles like Germans, or to turn America into a replica of Japan. Instead, the object is to examine a common problem facing two or more governments in order to learn how to develop a program that is applicable to immediate problems at home.

The program approach downgrades the significance of government in general; what government does is more relevant than how government is organized (Rose, 1985a). The focus is on particular functional areas or departments responsible for particular groups of programs, such as roads, health care, or museums.

Differences between the substance of programs, interests, expertise, and organizations create obstacles to the transfer of lessons between departments. The different departments into which government is divided functionally tend to be isolated from each other. Concurrently, similarities in problems and programs create links between departments in different places.

In the real world we would never expect a program to transfer without some adaptation, but equally we would not expect public officials to develop a major program in total ignorance of what is being done by counterparts elsewhere. Just as every government agency is vulnerable to events outside the agency's control, so too it may turn elsewhere for ideas about dealing with a common problem.

From a national perspective, state and local governments may be viewed as intervening variables, adapting programs to suit local or regional conditions but subject to outside influences. National governments, too, may be viewed as intervening variables between forces common to many advanced industrial societies, and "localized" (that is, national) responses (cf. Przeworski and Teune, 1970). Drawing a lesson does not deny the existence of obstacles to program transfers; it is about identifying such obstacles through a systematic analysis that locates action within "the architecture of complexity," involving a hierarchy of influences from the most place- and time-specific to the most general (Simon, 1969: 99ff).

Japan provides a striking and instructive example of the extent to which programs can be fungible. Many explanations of Japanese differences from the United States and Europe today are cultural, emphasizing the impermeability and inimitability of Japan. When Western countries forced Japan to resume commerce with the Western world in the mid-nineteenth century, the differences were greater still. Yet Japanese policymakers did not regard their distinctive national culture as a block on learning lessons from abroad. Instead, they saw technical backwardness as an imperative compelling the wholesale importation of lessons from abroad to enable Japan to catch up with foreign countries that used their superior technology to destroy Japan's previous isolation.

After the opening to the West, the Meiji authorities sent Japanese abroad to study programs in a variety of European countries and the United States (table 2.2). The Japanese did not seek to emulate a single nation; instead, individuals with a particular program interest were sent to a particular country identified as likely to have lessons for the modernization of Japan. The countries were chosen on the basis of limited information in Japan, prior contact in Asia, and international prestige. Sometimes, a Japanese traveler accidentally learned about a program subsequently emulated in Japan. The Japanese readiness to shop around for good lessons is illustrated by the experience of the army, which initially used France as a model, but abandoned it in favor of Prussia after the latter defeated the former in the Franco-Prussian war.

In order to draw lessons from abroad, Japan did not assume that it could copy exactly programs in effect elsewhere. In order to

TABLE 2.2

SOURCES OF LESSONS IN MEIJI JAPAN

SOURCE	PROGRAM	DATE
Britain	Navy	1869
	Telegraph system	1869
	Postal system	1872
	Postal savings	1875
France	Army	1869
	Primary school system	1872
	Judicial system	1872
	Tokyo police	1874
	Military police	1881
United States	National bank system	1872
	Primary school system	1879
	Sapporo Agricultural College	1879
Germany	Army	1878
Belgium	Bank of Japan	1882

SOURCE: Westney (1987: 13).

apply lessons successfully, it had to innovate as well as emulate (Westney, 1987: 224). For example, when introducing a national postal system along British lines, the Japanese could not use railways to carry mail, because this invention had yet to arrive. Instead, already existing networks of intercity runners were used to carry the mail from station to station. By 1905 the Japanese had sufficiently caught up with the West to win a war against Russia.

Japan's military defeat in World War II stimulated another round of lesson-drawing. Agency for International Development teams were established in Japan to facilitate study trips to the United States to observe the latest American public policy and economic practices. Each trip was planned with a specific functional goal in mind. The Japanese examined their own programs and institutions before visiting the United States. After returning home they were again encouraged to examine their own institutions in order to determine what could be adapted from what they had learned in the United States. As a participating official notes, "They did this quite well" (Nadler, 1984: 47). In the 1990s Japan continues to be at the center of another cycle in cross-national lesson-drawing, as America and Japan's neighbors in Asia seek to learn from Japan lessons that can enhance their own development (cf. Pempel, 1992).

The Need to Be Doubly Desirable

Lesson-drawing is about the means of policy, whether a program could transfer from one place to another; it cannot prescribe whether a program should be adopted. Yet ends come first in politics. The practical possibility of transferring a program is secondary to a decision about its desirability. Hence, a program must be doubly desirable, meeting both expert criteria for effective transfer and the politician's test of acceptable goals. Failure to meet either criterion can prevent the application of a lesson; however, neither is a permanent obstacle to lesson-drawing, for the dominant values in government are inherently unstable, and so too is technical knowledge.

What Is Lesson-drawing?

DISTINGUISHING PRACTICALITY FROM DESIRABILITY

To describe a program as "desirable" is ambiguous, for the meaning of the term differs with the type of evaluation being made. Prospective evaluation indicates whether or not a program is technically feasible, that is, whether a program in effect elsewhere could be realized here. A program that would fail to deliver as promised is technically undesirable.

However, evaluation by politicians stresses different criteria. A lesson is viewed as desirable only if it is consistent with the values and goals of those evaluating it. The technical feasibility of a new tax or labor law is less important than the values and interests of those affected by the measure. A prospective evaluation will be counterproductive if the expected impact is uncongenial to the governing party. Political feasibility also influences a politician's judgment of desirability. Is there a majority in favor of this program? If not, how would a program have to be altered to win majority support? If the results of the program are as promised, would we gain or lose support?

Proposals to reform election laws illustrate the distinction between technical and political feasibility. There are two very different ways of democratically electing representatives. Anglo-American countries use the simple plurality system; there is one winner, the candidate with the highest number of votes. But most democracies use a proportional representation system, in which a party is awarded seats in parliament in proportion to its share of the popular vote. The legislation necessary to change a country's electoral system from one method to the other is easily drafted, and it is technically possible to evaluate the prospective effects of a major change in the electoral system (see, e.g., Rose, 1983; Taagepera and Shugart, 1989: chapter 18).

However, technical feasibility does not make changing an electoral system politically desirable. Proposals for changing electoral laws usually fail the test of political desirability, for politicians enjoying power under the established electoral system have an interest in defending it. As long as those who would lose from changing electoral systems have the power to determine electoral laws, then a change in system is technically feasible but politically infeasible.

Logically, there are four ways of combining technical appraisals with political evaluations of desirability (figure 2.1). Two combinations show no difference in the outcome. If a program is deemed desirable by politicians and technical experts declare that it can transfer, then a lesson is doubly desirable. Equally, a program deemed undesirable by politicians and likely to fail if transferred will be rejected without hesitation, because it is doubly undesirable.

		DESIRABILITY	
		HIGH	LOW
PRACTICALITY	HIGH	Doubly desirable	Unwanted technical solution
	LOW	Siren call	Doubly rejected

FIGURE 2.1

DESIRABILITY AND PRACTICALITY OF TRANSFERRING PROGRAMS

Conflict arises when politicians are attracted to a program in effect elsewhere but prospective evaluation indicates that it would likely fail if adopted. This creates the problem of the *siren call*. In Greek mythology sirens lured sailors to steer in their direction, but the sirens' call actually lured sailors onto the rocks. If politicians adopt lessons solely on grounds of the desirability of goals, without regard to the feasibility of means, they run the risk of backing a shipwrecked program. Many of the proposals for the United States to copy Japanese economic practices are a statement of desire without any justification in technical analysis. Similarly, East European proclamations of the desire to adopt West European programs providing expensive social benefits are likely to collapse because post-communist societies currently lack the tax revenue to finance these benefits.

Academic policy analysts can prescribe the adoption of programs based on experience elsewhere and use their technical skills to demonstrate the feasibility of transferring their recommended programs. However, experts lack the political authority and legitimacy conferred by elective office. The decision about whether a lesson is adopted is in other hands. If the party in power views the ends or means of the proposed program as politically undesirable, then the lesson will be rejected as an unwanted technical solution.

INSTABILITY IN KNOWLEDGE AND VALUES

Judgments about the possibility and desirability of applying a lesson are time-bound. A statement that a proposed lesson is "not on" politically is a statement about current political preferences of the powers that be. However, the values of the governing majority are unstable. The technical judgments of experts are also subject to change through time.

Since politics involves the articulation of conflicting values, a lesson deemed desirable by some groups often meets opposition. But this also implies that if the government of the day is opposed to a program, there is minority support. And since the coalition in control of policymaking is usually a shifting one, any veto of a lesson on grounds of political undesirability cannot be treated as stable across time (cf. Sabatier, 1988).

In the course of time, shifts in electoral opinion can lead to a change in the party in control of government. Insofar as parties differ in their priorities and prohibitions, a lesson that was "not on" under one administration can become a priority for its successor. Changes in the leadership of the governing party can also make measures acceptable that were previously vetoed on political grounds. For example, in Britain in the 1980s a proposal could be dismissed as politically infeasible if the then prime minister, Margaret Thatcher, was known to oppose it. The replacement of Mrs. Thatcher by a different Conservative, John Major, created a situation in which it became possible to consider programs previously vetoed on political grounds.

Washington is an extreme example of instability because of conflicts between means and ends. Congress, the White House, bureaucrats, and interest groups operate in an institutional framework encouraging the articulation of support for a variety of conflicting programs. The resulting confusion produces a substantial degree of uncertainty about programs and goals. Given the need for a concurring majority in Congress and the executive branch, conflicting views may veto as politically infeasible the great bulk of technically feasible lessons. But it follows that during short periods, whether the 100-day "honeymoon" of a newly elected president or the duration of a political crisis, measures that have always been technically feasible suddenly become politically desirable too (cf. Kingdon, 1984; Polsby, 1984).

Evaluations of technical feasibility are also subject to change. The progressive nature of science can sooner or later make possible what was once technically infeasible. Scientific developments can also replace doubts and disagreements among scientists with certainty. A study of nineteenth-century efforts to agree on programs to prevent the spread of cholera found that the major obstacle was not a difference of political opinion about health goals; no government was in favor of cholera spreading. The problem was technical disagreement about the causes of the disease and the programs necessary to combat it. From this, Richard N. Cooper (1989: 237), himself a macroeconomist, concludes:

> All scientific parties to the debate were aware of the evidence, but the evidence was ambiguous and could be used to support conflicting theories. Epidemiology in the nineteenth century was much like economics in the twentieth century: a subject of intense public interest and concern, in which theories abounded but the scope for controlled experiments was limited.... So long as contention continued over the efficacy of different courses of action, it was impossible to get agreement among countries.

Once scientific discoveries ended technical disagreements about the most appropriate programs for combating cholera, governments on many continents could adopt similar programs.

Instability and uncertainty are arguments for caution in drawing lessons, but they also emphasize that even if a lesson does not appear politically desirable or technically feasible at a given time, rejection is not permanent. Rejection is no more and no less than a statement of what is possible here and now.

3

Searching for Lessons

What we learn depends upon what we do.

— Hugh Heclo

$\mathcal{D}$oing nothing is always a strategy that policymakers can follow. Inaction is efficient, for it requires the minimum investment of effort; low-level public officials can deliver services by routine. Ignoring routine activities allows an agency's head to devote time to urgent matters. When policymakers say that everything is satisfactory, what they mean is that everything seemed all right the last time that they looked. The decision rule is simple: "If it ain't broke, don't fix it."

Yet there comes a time in a program's life when dissatisfaction disrupts routine. Dissatisfaction can be signaled in many ways. Instead of offering support for a program, beneficiaries and their pressure groups can demand more or different services. The media can publicize complaints, political opponents are always ready to stir up discontent, and public opinion polls can register an increase in dissatisfaction. Officials in the field can report to their superiors that a program is not working as it used to. Budgets can go out of control.

Dissatisfaction stimulates policymakers to search for a solution, that is, actions that will reduce the gap between what is expected from a program and what government is doing. The status quo is not an option when a program that has worked in the past no longer generates satisfaction. Dissatisfaction is evidence that something has gone wrong, but it does not tell policymakers what to do. It simply emphasizes what not to do. Ignorance is the starting point of the search. Searching is a trial-and-error process in which many measures are considered and some are tried in hopes of finding a program that will restore satisfaction.

Policymakers have the choice of searching across time or space —or both. The simplest place for officials to search is their own past, in hopes of finding a program that has worked before. Another alternative is to speculate optimistically about the future. A search across space can explore what can be learned from responses to a similar problem in another setting.

Policymakers differ in the distance that they are prepared to travel in search of lessons. *Locals* concentrate on their immediate face-to-face environment, whether a government agency or a legislative chamber. By contrast, *cosmopolitans* are interested in what is happening in other agencies, in other states, and even in other countries (cf. Merton, 1957: 393ff). Most policymaking organizations will include both types of individual. Cosmopolitans can produce ideas based on a wide-ranging set of distant contacts. Locals can ask the equally important question for lesson-drawing: What does this mean for what we do here?

When searching, policymakers are not doing research as that term is understood in universities. Searching is instrumentally directed. Instead of seeking understanding for its own sake, harried policymakers seek to dispel dissatisfaction. Instead of new knowledge, policymakers prefer the assurance of doing what has worked before or worked somewhere else. As Cyert and March (1963: 121) emphasize:

> Problemistic search can be distinguished from both random curiosity and the search for understanding. It is distinguished from the former because it has a goal, and from the latter because it is interested in understanding only insofar as such understanding contributes to control. Problemistic search is engineering rather than pure science.

Lessons drawn depend on who searches, how a search is conducted, and how far the search extends across time and space. This chapter first considers the variety of individuals and organizations involved in the process of searching. It then outlines a behavioral model of policymaking as routine interrupted by dissatisfaction. The trial-and-error search for means of dispelling dissatisfaction is likely to start with what is near at hand, an organization's own past. Yet it can end on the other side of an ocean. Sources of ideas are both formal and informal, ranging from communities of experts linked by common professional concerns to intergovernmental agencies consciously trying to spread "best practice" programs around the world. Policymakers can evaluate what they find by examining trends in their own agency, by looking across international boundaries, or by looking simultaneously across time and space.

Who Searches?

The term *policymakers* invariably refers to a heterogeneous collection of officials and organizations concerned with one or more policy areas. Elected officials are involved because their values give direction to public policy and their endorsement is needed to legitimize the adoption of programs. The substantive expertise of non-elected officials is needed to formulate programs. A case study usually identifies policymakers by name, as if individual personality were all that mattered. Here, policymakers must be described in generic terms, according to their roles in the policy process and their offices in organizations.

Even though search is undertaken by individuals, searching is shaped by organizations. Organizations proceed differently than does an individual searching for knowledge. As Hedberg (1981: 6) remarks: "Organizations do not have brains, but they have cognitive systems and memories." An organization has institutionalized sources for receiving information, such as the reports of field staff routinely delivering its services. An organization employs officials with different forms of expertise: technical, social, economic, and political. An organization also has beneficiaries or clients and attracts pressure groups lobbying on their behalf.

An organization shapes how individual policymakers think, because holding an office—whether being elected a mayor or member of Congress or being appointed to a high post in an executive agency—imposes constraints on where individuals look and what individuals can do in their search for lessons (cf. Douglas, 1987). The formal and informal powers of an office define immediate responsibilities. Constraints within an organization define the programs that an individual within it can "sell" to colleagues and superiors. Political constraints outside an organization define what kinds of lessons can be adopted.

ELECTED OFFICEHOLDERS

Elected officials are first of all concerned with the constituency that elects them; a politician wants lessons that will benefit constituents. "All politics is local," declared Tip O'Neill, the former Speaker of the House of Representatives. Yet localities vary enormously. A city councillor can normally walk around his or her ward and know people on most streets; a state legislator can normally drive around a district in an hour or two.

When districts are as large as that of a member of the House of Representatives or the Senate, individual politicians have a lot of room for choice about where to look for votes and programs. Many districts are large and heterogeneous; more than half a million people live in the average district of a member of the House of Representatives, and five million in a senator's constituency. Fenno's (1978: 28) study of members of Congress shows that there is a "tremendous amount of uncertainty surrounding the House member's view of his or her electoral situation." To a significant extent, a member of Congress can construct a constituency according to taste.

Second, because policymaking is a collective activity, elected representatives must look to other elected officials. A politician who simply says what constituents want to hear will tend to be ignored by legislative colleagues who represent different districts with different audiences. In order to convert a lesson into a law as well as a speech, a legislator must discuss ideas with others. This discussion is a process of mutual learning and a prelude to bargaining. A city councillor learns that other wards are different, by race, income, and other concerns, than his or her ward. A state legislator learns about urban-rural differences.

Arrival in Washington exposes members of Congress to ideas and information from throughout the nation; however egoistic a senator is, he or she learns that there are ninety-nine other egos of equal size in the Senate. Many concerns of government, ranging from defense to social security, are common nationwide. To get action on behalf of their districts, elected representatives must aggregate local interests with those of other districts. Working inside the Washington beltway tends to nationalize the outlook of elected representatives (Arnold, 1979), as they learn that programs of special benefit to their own constituents may not be popular nationwide.

Party is a third influence on the education of elected officials. Searching for programs can follow partisan lines. Even when partisan values are weak, the tendency of legislatures to organize along party lines means that individual politicians are regularly in contact with partisan colleagues from whom they can learn about the problems of other parts of their city, state, or nation.

The presidency is uniquely positioned to learn about problems and search for solutions. As the elected leader of the nation, the president receives streams of complaints and suggestions for action. As the head of the executive branch, the president can draw on the collective knowledge of experts in federal agencies. Yet because the president is elected by the most heterogeneous coalition in American society, the White House is also very sensitive to criticism from many sources. The lessons a president learns may concentrate on the presentation and politics of policies.

Even though the collective nature of decision making forces politicians to learn about programs outside their immediate concern, the development of a broader outlook normally stops at the water's edge. Elected American officials have little or no contact with events, institutions, or individuals in other countries. Nor is there much incentive to have such contacts, since foreigners do not vote in American elections and the votes of foreign legislators are of no significance in a calculus of support in Congress. When notice is taken of foreigners, the aim may be to secure domestic advantage rather than to learn lessons for positive policymaking. Japan-bashing is an extreme example of using another country in order to score domestic political points.

Legislators in smaller countries with bigger neighbors are much more likely, from necessity or self-defense, to learn from foreign experience. Canadian policymakers routinely receive much information about American programs from media that circulate across North America. Although Canada covers a vast expanse from the Atlantic to the Pacific and the Arctic, the great bulk of its population is concentrated closer to the American border than to the capital, Ottawa (cf. Duchacek, 1984; Hoberg, 1991).

In smaller European democracies, elected officials recognize that decisions taken outside their national boundaries by governments of bigger and richer nations influence their own political fortunes. The experience of war is a reminder of how open borders are between European nations. The capitals of major European nations are far closer together than are New York and Los Angeles, and the distance between Paris and Brussels or London and Bonn is less than that between Washington and Boston. Many European politicians know at least one foreign language, often English, and are attentive to what is happening in both the United States and other countries of Europe. Leading politicians in member-states of the European Community have many programs with both a national and an international dimension.

NON-ELECTED EXPERTS

Most high-level civil servants are doubly specialists: They are experts in a substantive field of public policy and they know a lot about how government works. Civil servants are usually recruited on the basis of specialist knowledge, for example, in geodesic survey work, as public health professionals, or as tax lawyers. In the course of a government career, officials gain experience about the practice and theory of programs for which they are responsible. Whereas presidential or gubernatorial appointees may hold office for only two years, career officials expect to spend at least twenty years in an agency. They thus accumulate a large fund of experience about programs.

Officials understand the procedures for operating programs, knowledge essential for designing new programs. They also understand the political interests supporting the status quo. As long as there is satisfaction, this may make officials cautious about proposing change. However, once dissatisfaction creates a demand for action, then public officials can use their specialist skills to search for lessons that will produce programs effective in practice and acceptable to the prevailing political majority.

Pressure-group officials have no formal position within government, but the political influence of their organizations causes both elected officials and civil servants to turn to them for information necessary to form a majority coalition. Pressure groups claim a distinctive advantage in being able to instruct officials inside government in how their members perceive public programs. Pressure groups are also repositories of knowledge about programs in operation throughout the United States and, sometimes, about programs abroad. They can thus claim attention as sources of ideas about how to change programs, as well as wielders of political clout.

Groups advocating the same interest in different states are likely to promote the same types of activities, because their members—whether teachers, utility companies, or construction unions—share common concerns. Pressure groups operating in a state capital are often chapters of nationwide organizations with centrally defined programs and are capable of coordinating interstate action. Insofar as nationwide interest groups succeed in promoting legislation in different states, the result is what Clemens (1990: 6) describes as "secondhand laws.... One cannot assume that the most important forces behind policy events in a given state come from within that state." In other words, the crucial word in the name of an organization such as the Missouri State Teachers Association is not Missouri but *teachers*.

Policy entrepreneurs combine commitment to program goals with long service in government. In the course of a career, a policy entrepreneur may hold a civil service job, receive an appointment as a special assistant to a Cabinet secretary, work for a member of Congress, and head an agency as a presidential appointee. Many also have had university connections. Policy entrepreneurs are usually very well informed about the substance and the politics of programs. Their concern with a special subject, whether social security or atomic energy regulation, leads them to build up a nationwide or international network of contacts that are a source of ideas for new programs and of evidence to support the lessons that they choose to draw (cf. Marmor with Fellman, 1986; Doig and Hargrove, 1987).

In the process of policymaking, elected and non-elected officials often search in complementary ways. Politicians are likely to give priority to demands that something be done to advance goals, using examples elsewhere to fuel a demand for action. They are less likely to be interested in lessons that specify the details of programs. Career officials usually give priority to the administrative feasibility of transferring a program from one setting to another. The time-horizons of the two groups also tend to differ. Members of Congress are up for reelection every two years, and White House staff may feel that everything hinges on the latest public opinion poll. By contrast, non-elected officials have a time-horizon of years or decades; they can draw lessons from past experience and they expect to be around after a new program comes into effect. For a lesson to be put into effect, elected politicians and career officials must both be involved, for even though the ship of state has only one tiller, it is steered by two pairs of hands (Rose, 1987b).

Dissatisfaction: the Stimulus to Search

A necessary condition of lesson-drawing is that policymakers want to learn something that they do not already know. Capturing the attention of politicians in power is not easy. Power can be defined as "the ability to talk instead of listen, the ability to afford not to learn" (Deutsch, 1963: 111). Yet no representative and responsive government can be indifferent to a rising tide of political dissatisfaction.

Policymakers do not have the time or the knowledge to be maximizers, continuously seeking an ideal policy. In Herbert Simon's (1979: 503) term, they are *satisficers*. The relation between aspiration and achievement determines when a search starts and when it stops. As long as a program's outcome matches aspirations, there is satisfaction; it can run by routine. However, if a gap appears between aspirations and achievements, this creates dissatisfaction, and it is dissatisfaction that stimulates a search for measures to close the gap. Satisficing behavior can account for policymakers starting to search, and then stopping.

The gap between achievement and aspirations can be closed by raising the level of achievement, for example, spending more money on an existing program. But if more of the same does not produce satisfaction, then it may be necessary to lower aspirations, or search elsewhere. The more intense the dissatisfaction, the greater the pressure to search far and wide.

RUNNING BY ROUTINE

In an era of big government, most public agencies operate by routine. Otherwise, the everyday services of government—education, health care, the payment of social security benefits, and the collection of garbage—could not be delivered.

The great majority of public officials are not concerned with learning fresh lessons. Many are rule-bound bureaucrats trained to follow formal procedures and regulations laid down by statute and informal routines developed by colleagues. Technicians have the skill to make routine adjustments in standard operating procedures, but they are not expected to develop new policies. Only a small percentage of civil servants are at the policymaking level; typically they are expert professionals.

In the economy of administration, busy policymakers have a strong incentive to ignore the routine activities of their subordinates, for time is limited, and the political system always generates more demands than there is time to respond to them. As Simon

(1978: 13) explains: "In a world where attention is a major scarce resource, information may be an expensive luxury, for it may turn our attention from what is important to what is unimportant. We cannot afford to attend to information simply because it is there." Policymakers can ignore programs—as long as routine activities appear to be producing satisfaction.

A gap between a program's aspiration and its achievement is an ambiguous cue to action. It can be interpreted as evidence of a need to raise achievements or to lower aspirations. For example, in the early 1970s a rise in unemployment and inflation created a gap between aspirations and achievements; the results were labeled "intolerable." Yet the persistence of high rates of unemployment and inflation led to a lowering of aspiration levels, so that the gap was closed as levels once deemed unsatisfactory became widely evaluated as the best that could be achieved in difficult circumstances. Policymakers have a dynamic set of goals, changing their definition of what a program should achieve in the light of experience, thus altering whether a program is considered a problem or operating routinely (Cohen and Axelrod, 1984; Dery, 1982).

BECOMING DISSATISFIED

The development of new ideas to improve public programs is not sufficient to disrupt routine. Heclo's (1974: 305) study of the role of administrative officials in promoting policies emphasizes: "What officials have rarely been able to do is to fire up, by themselves, sufficient political steam to create new policies." Before a new program can be considered, the status quo must be assessed as unsatisfactory.

The definition of a satisfactory, or at least a "not unsatisfactory," program is problematic. The aspirations against which achievements are judged are not given, but are social constructions.

> A policy problem is a political condition that does not meet some standard. Problems can be appraised in the light of many different political principles....
> Public problems are not just "out there" waiting to be dealt

with. Policymaking is not simply problem-solving. It is also a matter of setting up and defining problems in the first place. (Anderson, 1978: 19–20)

Dissatisfaction can have many causes. First of all, there is palpable and inescapable evidence of what is colloquially labeled failure—for example, a sharp rise in inflation or unemployment. An OECD study, *Why Economic Policies Change Course*, concludes that it is not the promise of greater benefits that causes change in programs but growing evidence that a program is "likely to result in discontinuities and dislocations, such as a collapse of the exchange rate and accelerating inflation, with severe costs that are economic, political and social" (Organisation for Economic Cooperation and Development, 1988: 12).

Values are a second influence on the level of dissatisfaction. Political values influence whether there is a consensus (whether it expresses satisfaction or dissatisfaction) about conditions. Poverty, for example, has always existed in America, and government has always maintained a number of antipoverty programs. However, it took leadership by President Lyndon Johnson to create dissatisfaction with the then-existing levels of poverty and generate an effective political demand for a "war" on poverty. Dissensus is routinely shown in the response to the publication of figures of rising corporate profits. These will be interpreted as satisfactory by pro-business politicians but stimulate dissatisfaction among liberals and social democrats.

Expert values can also lead to a given condition being labeled as a problem. A recurring motif of the environmental movement is that environmental conditions long taken for granted ought to be considered "unsatisfactory" or even "catastrophic." Environmental campaigners propagate standards and values that promote dissatisfaction with present conditions in order to create a demand for new programs that will impose more stringent standards against pollution.

Change in the policy environment causing the effects of programs to alter without any change in laws or policy directives is a third cause of dissatisfaction. For example, the increasing longevity of the population causes a big increase in the number and cost of services provided to the elderly under Medicare, and this in turn pushes up the federal deficit. Concurrently, advances in medical technology lead to more elaborate and expensive ways of caring for health. The result is a major increase in dissatisfaction with the cost of health-care programs, both public and private.

As government has become more involved in a greater variety of increasingly complex activities, so programs become more vulnerable to change from more remote, uncontrollable, and unpredictable sources. The expertise of experts is less effective in providing policy prescriptions, and this increases dissatisfaction. As two experienced Washington policy analysts note: "Economists remain woefully unable to predict how the economy will react to policy changes. To a far greater extent than in the past individuals who must make the difficult economic choices in Washington are in the dark" (Aho and Levinson, 1988: 8).

Electoral competition is a fourth source of dissatisfaction. The division between a Republican White House and a Democratic Congress and factionalism and freelancing in both parties give politicians opportunities to stir up dissatisfaction. When public opinion polls register a slump in the popularity of elected officials, this is a stimulus to search for measures to regain popularity. Competition between parties can lead the administration to seek new programs that it can claim credit for before they are promoted by their opponents.

Dissatisfaction may even be imported from abroad. American policy entrepreneurs can point to Japanese achievements as a reason for dissatisfaction with America's industrial policy. In Canada, pressure groups monitor activities of American pressure groups, seeking to import dissatisfaction by pointing to activities in America as a reason why Ottawa should act.

Dissatisfaction works by sanctions. The stimulus for search arises less from the uncertain promise of benefits than from the certain threat of pain if something is not done. Policymakers who do not heed evidence of dissatisfaction risk losing support or losing office. As policymakers' awareness of dissatisfaction increases, the cost of inaction rises (Rose, 1972). Dissatisfaction stimulates search with the argument "You can't afford not to."

SEARCHING FOR SATISFACTION

A symbolic gesture is the simplest and easiest response to a problem. At a minimum, symbolic gestures show that politicians care about a difficulty. For example, if a natural disaster strikes a region, the head of the agency nominally responsible can fly there to demonstrate concern. If symbolic gestures fail to produce satisfaction, this is an indication that there is something materially wrong with a program.

In searching for satisfaction, policymakers do not have the time to look everywhere and consider every possibility; they follow the line of least resistance. The basic decision rule is: *In response to signals of dissatisfaction, start searching near at hand.* The definition of proximity is subjective. Proximity depends on cognition; what is already known will be appreciated before what is unfamiliar (cf. Cyert and March, 1963: 121ff).

An organization's own past is normally the first place to search for lessons. An agency develops an institutional memory of programs that have brought satisfaction in the past. Past experience can be incorporated in laws that give an agency the authority to spend extra money in the face of difficulties, for example, responding to a drought by making emergency payments to farmers, or releasing funds for public works at the start of a recession. Dissatisfaction also encourages pressure groups to lobby an agency to adopt suggestions that it previously rejected. The stronger the signs of dissatisfaction, the less likely it is that an organization's existing knowledge will be sufficient. When a problem is unprecedented, then an organization's past cannot offer a solution.

When past experience fails, an agency can speculate about the future unencumbered by experience. Theoretical economics, for example, draws policy prescriptions for future action without regard to historical experience or national contexts. However, advice that is purely speculative may be treated skeptically by policymakers facing concrete problems and requiring measures that can be clearly set out in laws and administrative regulations.

Searching for lessons across space is the third major alternative. The scope of a search is a function of the problem at hand. County government officials are likely to look to other counties in the same state for lessons, on the assumption that they have most in common with their neighbors. But when a big city is the only place in a state with inner-city problems, its mayor must look to cities in other states. American state officials are likely to turn to neighboring states or to states viewed as in the vanguard in dealing with a problem. When there is no domestic variation in a national problem, for example, federal social security, national policymakers are driven to look abroad for lessons.

Trial and error is the best way to describe the search for something that will dispel dissatisfaction. When dissatisfaction is high, the pressure to act is great—even if what is done has a substantial probability of failure. The first actions taken may be hurried, without any theoretical or empirical justification, and fail to dispel dissatisfaction. Yet trying and failing can become a source of ideas about what to try next. Mistakes need not be a waste of resources; they can be considered the tuition charge that an agency pays in order to learn how to deal with dissatisfaction.

A trial-and-error approach makes it possible for an organization to learn from its own actions as well as from the experience of others. This is possible as long as an organization is open to feedback about its actions. Feedback about the impact of a trial program can then be evaluated. Insofar as feedback indicates continuing dissatisfaction, then as long as mistakes are corrigible, another program can be adopted in a disjointed serial effort to remove initial deficiencies (cf. Braybrooke and Lindblom, 1963).

As policymakers search farther and farther afield, the response to dissatisfaction becomes more indeterminate and nonlinear. The process is indeterminate because there are no fixed rules guaranteeing success. It is nonlinear because if steps in one direction fail to produce satisfaction, then policymakers can search in another direction for something that satisfices.

Informal and Formal Sources of Ideas

In searching for lessons, policymakers make use of both formal and informal networks disseminating information, advice, and money. The great majority of public officials are part of a formal network including other agencies addressing the same set of problems. Internationally, there are formal institutions. The European Community, for example, has some binding authority over twelve national governments. And an organization such as the International Monetary Fund can make acceptance of its lessons a condition of a government's receiving financial support.

The distinction between formal and informal advice is often blurred, for few intergovernmental bodies have the power to mandate their recommendations for program change unilaterally. Federalism does not empower the federal secretary of education to tell school boards or principals how to run local schools; it simply enables federal officials to offer advice and, if Congress appropriates money, cash incentives too. The European Community has formal authority in a limited number of fields, but its decisions are not imposed in a vacuum; they are the outcome of political bargaining between policymakers representing the national governments that constitute its membership.

COMMUNITIES OF EXPERTS

Most non-elected officials are experts in a substantive area of public policy. The majority of state government officials have a graduate professional degree as well as a college diploma and belong to at least two professional associations (Grady and Chi, 1990: 11); for example, a public health official will normally have a medical degree and a degree in health administration. Professional education is the start of a process of socialization into a community sharing common interests and knowledge. Information, ideas, and values are disseminated through specialist publications, state and national meetings, and organizations promoting professional best practice.

Communities are informal because they exist independently of government agencies; membership cuts across the boundaries of federalism, the public and private sectors, and may even bridge international boundaries. Civil engineers, medical doctors, accountants, and computer experts regularly meet others with similar training but a different employer to discuss matters of common concern. The community usually communicates through a formal professional association and informally by telephone, letter, and face-to-face meetings.

Expertise—that is, a core body of knowledge and skills acquired through professional training and experience in applying principles and theories—is the claim of a professional. Expertise can be found in the so-called hard sciences, such as aeronautical engineering, in the so-called soft sciences, such as social work, or in fields where professional practice is considered more important than academic theories, such as law, accountancy, and management. Even though many members of an expert community may be employed by government, their expertise does not depend on official position but on knowledge and professional skills. Knowledge by itself does not provide the authority to commit government to act, but the collective knowledge of a community is a major resource for lessons about how government might respond to dissatisfaction.

When seeking ideas, professionals can turn to an expert community as well as draw on government experience. A public health official will learn ideas in medical journals and scientific meetings as well as in agency meetings and bureaucratic reports. Insofar as diseases have common attributes regardless of country, officials can read with interest the results of research and practice in foreign countries. Epidemiologists are particularly concerned with drawing lessons across time and space, because they study causes of differences in the incidence of disease between regions and nations in order to develop new programs to reduce disease.

Expert communities create links between different levels of government. A community of specialists in education can be found in every city. The state level brings together local school officials, officials of the state department of education, a variety of academics employed in teacher training and evaluation, and a few free-floating experts. This community has much in common, for education programs are usually determined at state and local level. Leaders at the state level are usually part of the national community of education policy and administration, where differences between programs are more likely. In turn, some members of the national community are active in the international community of education policy experts. Although the level varies, the subject matter is constant: education programs. When dissatisfaction arises at home, this community of knowledgeable experts can be drawn on for lessons.

Although experts share common intellectual interests, training, and methods, they may not share a common set of political values. Since policy advice combines extra-professional value judgments with technical knowledge of possibilities, experts often disagree in the advice that they give. Hence, it is wrong to suggest that experts form a network that can "authoritatively" define policies on the basis of "shared" beliefs and standards (P. Haas, 1990: 24; E. Haas, 1990). Even Ph.D.s in the same subject can differ along political lines. Disagreements are institutionalized in the legal system, for challenges to public policy in the courts set lawyers for the plaintiff against the government's lawyers. Differences in what is perceived as knowledge can also be found across national lines. For example, American environmentalists "have tended to redefine environmental protection as health protection and health protection as prevention of cancer," thus labeling more substances as carcinogenic than do governments in Europe (Hoberg, 1986: 365).

Even though economics is often thought to be the most positivistic or "value-free" of the social sciences, surveys of economists in the United States and Europe consistently show substantial differences of opinion about scientific propositions and about values relevant for deriving lessons for public policy (cf. Kearl et al., 1979; Frey et al., 1984; Ricketts and Shoesmith, 1990). When economists are asked questions about whether inflation is a monetary problem, about the power of trade unions, and about buying and selling human organs for transplant operations, the divisions are so nearly equal that the median respondent is literally a "don't know" (table 3.1).

When government agencies employ officials with different types of expertise, such as lawyers, economists, and scientists, political conflicts can arise within an agency about which expert values should determine policies. In an environmental protection agency, ecologists are likely to value the preservation of nature as priceless. Lawyers can approach environmental problems in terms

TABLE 3.1

DIFFERENCES OF OPINION AMONG BRITISH ECONOMISTS

	AGREE	DON'T KNOW	DIS- AGREE
Permitting trade in human organs for transplant purposes would be economically efficient	37%	24%	37%
Wage-price controls should be used to control inflation	34	14	51
Effluent taxes are better for pollution control than imposing pollution ceilings	59	16	25
The money supply is a more important target than interest rates for monetary policy	29	28	42
Inflation is primarily a monetary phenomenon	42	17	41
The power of trade unions is not a significant economic problem	43	18	39

SOURCE: Martin Ricketts and Edward Shoesmith, *British Economic Opinion*. London: Institute of Economic Affairs Research Monograph 45, 1990, figure 9.

of what the law says and disregard the costs of obeying the law. By contrast, economists calculate the costs and benefits of everything, making tradeoffs between environmental pollution and economic growth before seeing whether or not the law agrees with their calculations (Kelman, 1981).

The divergence of opinions among groups of experts and between different forms of expertise gives politicians much more freedom of action. Elected officials searching for lessons prefer advice from those whose overall political outlook is consistent with their own. As long as there are diverse political outlooks, there will always be some experts sharing values consistent with politicians in power.

INTERGOVERNMENTAL LINKS WITHIN AND BETWEEN NATIONS

The government of the United States consists of more than 80,000 "governments," that is, authorities with distinctive functional and territorial competences. When account is taken of divisions by subject matter within what is nominally a single government (for example, between different federal departments and agencies in Washington or between bureaus within a large federal department or between different functional departments within a city hall), the number of institutions within government rises toward a million. In a European country, "governments" are numbered in the hundreds or the thousands.

The great majority of public policy problems are common to a number of agencies with different jurisdictions in a nation. In the federal system, the variety of institutions creates a laboratory in which each state and city may try different programs or apply federal guidelines in different ways. Officials in cities and states know where to search when a problem arises: They can turn to cities and states with similar problems, resources, and political values. Informal communication networks make it easy to draw on the experience of friends and neighbors (cf. Wright, 1988; Brudney et al., 1990: table 7; Wright and Hebert, 1990: table 4).

It is also possible to search through vertical links between agencies addressing the same problem at different levels of government. Typically, responsibility for delivering services is given to local or state agencies, and responsibility for broad lines of policy and much funding rests at a higher level. Within a given field, officials in Washington can look to service-delivery agencies in the states and cities to learn what is happening at the grass roots. When dissatisfaction arises, agencies at the grass roots can look for lessons to Washington and other national centers. The federal courts play a special role in enforcing federal standards.

Moving ideas between nations is more difficult, for most international institutions lack the authority to compel national governments to adopt programs that they recommend. International brokers of ideas depend on national conditions in member countries becoming so unsatisfactory that their governments are driven to look abroad for lessons, as well as on the positive attraction of their information and advice.

The Organization for Economic Cooperation and Development (OECD) is a prime example of an "ideas-mongering" international institution. It does not have the authority to issue laws and regulations that member countries must obey. Nor does it disburse large sums of money to encourage new programs in member states. It does, however, regularly compile statistical information about economic and social conditions in twenty-four advanced industrial nations. The data can be used to construct league tables that rank countries high or low in economic growth, social policy expenditures, and indicators of social well-being. In countries that rank low in these tables, pressure groups can use the data to stimulate dissatisfaction and demands for action. Countries that rank high have lessons to offer.

The ideas-mongering activities of OECD are carried out through expert committees concerned with topics such as economic growth, taxation, employment, and social security. National governments routinely send officials to attend specialist meetings to exchange ideas with policymakers from other countries. When member countries identify a common concern, the multinational staff of OECD prepares papers that diagnose the problem and identify programs that produce satisfaction. From these case studies lessons are distilled that other nations can choose to adopt if they wish. However, OECD has neither incentives nor sanctions to make a country change a program. The push to change must come from national governments.

Among advanced industrial nations, the European Community (EC) is unique in being an intergovernmental body that not only moves ideas but also has a small but growing amount of authority over member-states. The Treaty of Rome and subsequent agreements bind EC countries to accept Community directives on issues concerning trade, industry, employment, agriculture, and associated topics. It also gives the Community a small but significant amount of revenue, most of which is spent on agricultural and regional programs. The Community's creation of a Single European Market is drawing member states closer together.

In order to establish Community regulations, there must be a common fund of knowledge about programs already in effect in each country. The European Commission, the Brussels-based administrative arm of the EC, has divisions concerned with agriculture, industry, regional policy, trade, finance, environment, science, social affairs, education, and so forth. Brussels initiatives must be supported by the Council of Ministers, which represents national ministries in areas in which the EC claims concurrent jurisdiction. When examining programs across the twelve countries of the Community, national ministries can puzzle over differences that they observe, and ask: Could or should another program work in our country, or could our program work elsewhere?

Community policies start from the assumption that programs in effect in one country could be transferred to other member states. A collective EC decision can compel member states to adopt common goals that take into account standards in other member countries. To date, the European Commission, the executive body of the Community, has emphasized common goals rather than seeking to mandate a uniform program from Denmark to Italy and from Ireland to Germany's border with Poland. But it leaves decisions about what a country learns from others to each government. As long as a national program is not incompatible with fundamental Community principles, then it is deemed acceptable. National dissatisfaction, not a push from Brussels, is meant to be the trigger for seeking lessons from other countries.

The World Bank and the International Monetary Fund (IMF) are distinctive in offering countries money as well as information. The World Bank's broad aim is to encourage the economic and social development of less-developed nations. It gives loans and grants for agriculture, industry, education, and social development to more than one hundred African, Asian, Middle Eastern, Latin American, and East European nations.

By definition, governments in developing nations are searching for means of raising their living standards and in some sense "catching up" with more-developed nations. In order to reduce the gap between achievements and aspirations, they need to find new ways of doing things. They may look to other nations at a similar level of development but with faster rates of growth, or to more advanced nations. The World Bank serves two purposes: It acts as a clearinghouse for lessons in development, and it offers money to finance new programs.

The IMF has both a carrot and a stick to encourage countries to accept its lessons. Its principal contact within a country is the country's central bank; responsibility for foreign exchange makes a central bank look abroad to see how similar institutions operate. A country wanting to learn more about international practices in monetary policy, taxation, and public expenditure can turn to the IMF for lessons based on its fund of experience. As long as a nation's finances are not in difficulty, applying lessons is at its discretion.

When a country has great difficulty in financing foreign exchange and debts, it turns to the IMF for a loan. To secure the loan, a national government must agree to conditions intended to restore financial solvency. These conditions involve programs that the IMF has prescribed to other nations. There is no doubt that IMF lessons for monetary policy can be applied across time and space; critics of the IMF accept this. Their complaint is that IMF lessons are only too effective in stopping national governments from promoting programs that the critics favor.

Evaluating Lessons across Time and Space

Searching for information about programs elsewhere is useful but incomplete; what is learned must then be evaluated. Evaluation involves comparison against observed outcomes at another point in time or space. Lesson-drawing goes well beyond static or parochial forms of evaluation; it involves comparison across both space and time (figure 3.1). When evaluation indicates complete satisfaction, then there is no need to draw a lesson. Insofar as comparison stimulates dissatisfaction, it is a step in the process of lesson-drawing.

The simplest form of evaluation compares the present performance of an existing program with current aspirations. Since public programs normally persist for many years, the current aspirations of policymakers incorporate the experience of the past instead of an idealized maximum. Because policymakers responsible for a program have a bias toward satisfaction, there is a tendency to adjust aspirations down or up as performance alters (Cyert and March, 1963: 123). As long as achievements and aspirations can be matched, the result is *routine satisfaction*. There is no need to search for a new measure. Policymakers can ignore what is happening elsewhere.

		ACROSS TIME	
		NO	YES
ACROSS SPACE	NO	Routine satisfaction	Trend analysis
	YES	Comparative statics: league tables	Comparative dynamics: lesson-drawing

FIGURE 3.1
EVALUATION ACROSS TIME AND SPACE

Evaluating a current program by its past performance is a standard method of comparison within an agency. Economic and social statistics facilitate *trend analysis;* each monthly, quarterly, or annual report normally contains a figure or table comparing current conditions with past performance. Trend analysis avoids the difficulties of agreeing on an absolute (and potentially impossible) standard of success. The important question is whether a program is doing better or worse than a month or a year ago.

Trend analysis assumes that any changes in programs are incremental. As long as changes are at the expected rate and positive (for example, if the economy registers continuing growth), then the trend reinforces satisfaction. If trends are negative (for example, the rate of economic growth is slowing down or the economy is contracting), this stimulates dissatisfaction. A reversal of direction is often a cause for concern, for example, if the unemployment or inflation rate starts rising rather than falling.

Whereas incremental trends are small, comparison across space can identify programs that differ in magnitude or in kind. *Comparative statics* compare an agency's program with what is done elsewhere. A league table is produced in which different cities, states, or countries are ranked from top to bottom by a common measure. A high school principal can compare the percentage going to college with the record of other high schools in the same school district; a state education official can compare state expenditures on education with those of forty-nine other states; and a federal official can compare education achievement test scores with those of other advanced industrial nations.

The interpretation of league tables is problematic. In sports, only one team can rank first, but in public policy it is not necessary to rank first to achieve satisfaction. If that were the standard, then all but one would be deemed unsatisfactory. However, if the median is used to discriminate between satisfactory and unsatisfactory performance, then half the cases will be satisfactory. Officials who find their performance ranked below average can argue that other conditions are not equal. A high school in an inner city does not expect to have as high a proportion of pupils going to college as a school in a wealthy suburb, and educators in a poor state may be satisfied with a lower level of expenditure than educators in a rich state. In cross-national comparisons, even though Americans may expect to rank first in everything, a sixth-place ranking is not evidence of failure if comparison covers 150 countries of the United Nations.

Comparative evaluation of public programs can focus on program outputs or outcomes. Outputs are normally measured in terms of public expenditure. Social security programs can be compared in terms of the amount of money spent in cash transfers to the old and needy, or as a percentage of gross domestic product. This is reasonable as increased cash income for the elderly is the outcome of a social security program. Cash outputs are also used as proxy indicators of benefits in fields such as education and health; however, the output of these services is not cash paid to pupils or sick people but payments to teachers, doctors, and hospitals.

Outcome measures focus on social conditions; the purpose of an education program is to educate youths, and of health care to sustain physical well-being. A comparison of health in terms of expenditure and the health of the population illustrates the importance of the distinction between program outputs and outcomes (table 3.2). If American health programs are evaluated in terms of outputs, the United States leads advanced industrialized societies. It spends 11.8 percent of its gross domestic product on health care, double the proportion in Britain and two-thirds more than the average of other major nations. Given American wealth, it also spends more than twice as much per person on health care, even after adjustment for differences in the purchasing power of national currencies. The high level of American health expenditure occurs without a formal program of national health insurance because federal laws and employer practices make expenditure a joint responsibility of the government, not-for-profit agencies, and profitmaking bodies.

When health is evaluated by the condition of the population, the United States ranks last rather than first. Infant mortality in Japan is less than half that in the United States, and in Sweden is almost a third lower than in the United States. Life expectancy for older citizens is normally higher in other major countries, too; the United States ranks fifth among the eight nations reviewed in table 3.2.

League-table evaluations are useful knowledge, but they are insufficient as a basis for action. A negative evaluation indicates that a program here is not as effective as programs elsewhere. This is particularly so in the case of health, where the amount of money allocated is not the problem; America outspends but underperforms other nations. A league table can stimulate a search to learn what other countries are doing to achieve a better outcome. But

TABLE 3.2

HEALTH PROGRAM OUTPUTS AND OUTCOMES

	OUTPUTS			OUTCOMES	
	PUBLIC EXPENDITURES % GDP	TOTAL EXPENDITURES % GDP	TOTAL EXPENDITURES $ PER CAPITA	INFANT MORTALITY PER 1000	LIFE EXPECTANCY (IN YEARS)
Japan	4.8	6.7	1035	4.6	84.3
Sweden	8.3	8.8	1361	5.8	83.4
Canada	6.5	8.7	1683	7.2	83.2
France	6.7	8.7	1274	7.5	83.7
Germany	6.3	8.2	1232	7.5	81.9
Britain	5.3	5.8	836	8.4	81.2
Italy	5.2	7.6	1050	8.9	82.4
United States	4.5	11.8	2354	9.7	82.5

SOURCE: OECD, *OECD in Figures.* Supplement to *OECD Observer*, no. 158 (1989): 16–17; 170 (1991): 46–47.

NOTE: Public expenditures date normally from 1986; total expenditures from 1989. Per capita dollar amounts adjusted for purchasing power parity. Life expectancy is for females age 60.

studying what is done elsewhere is only one step in answering the instrumental question: How can health care be improved here?

Lesson-drawing is an exercise in *comparative dynamics*; evaluation of current practice elsewhere leads to lessons for changing the future here. Comparative dynamics is about closing the performance gap by catching up with the performance of leaders. The initial step is explaining why one place ranks low compared to another. Sometimes differences can be explained by unequal resources; for example, a league table of social security benefits will show that rich countries usually pay a higher level of benefits. Often, it is easier to identify the size of the gap than to decide what lesson can be drawn for public policy.

The logic of satisficing sets no limit on the distance covered in a sequential search across time and space. Searching one's own past is the starting point but usually not the conclusion. Static comparisons call attention to how programs differ, implying that two countries different today are likely to remain different tomorrow. Comparative dynamics focuses on the contingent steps necessary to transfer a program from one place to another. Achievements elsewhere are used to force forward the critical analytic question: Under what circumstances and to what extent can a program that already works there work here in the future?

4

Searching across Time

Across contemporary national boundaries and backward through time, both the elementary "housekeeping" problems and the complex problems of organizing power and influence recur.

What is striking is that these are problems we keep working at in highly developed democracies, and they are as well problems of the Buganda Kingdom in Africa, of the young republics of Vietnam and Indonesia, of Imperial Rome, of Charlemagne's empire.

— James W. Fesler

$\mathcal{D}$iagnosing the cause of a problem is a logical precondition of drawing lessons for action. Current dissatisfaction cannot be understood by examining only the present. Whereas action is future-oriented, diagnosis requires searching the past to understand why a program that worked before no longer produces satisfaction. No point in time contains its own explanation. As Schumpeter (1946: 1) argued: "In order to understand the religious events from 1520 to 1530 or the political events from 1790 to 1800 or the developments in painting from 1900 to 1910, you must survey a period of much wider span. Not to do so is the hallmark of dilettantism."

What is true in the *longue durée* of history is equally true in contemporary government. The federal deficit of the 1990s cannot be understood without knowing how the federal deficit was created in the 1980s. To understand demands for affirmative action to promote racial equality requires knowing about the legacy of discrimination that extends back to the era of slavery.

Searching the past can extend across both time and space. James Fesler (1959: 215) explains why: Many of the problems of government are perennial. Insofar as problems recur, new democracies in Eastern Europe may turn to older democracies in Western Europe or North America for lessons about how to develop representative institutions. Soldiers and diplomats are particularly interested in searching the past of other countries in order to learn from the mistakes of other nations rather than learn through military defeat.

Policymakers are inheritors before they are choosers; as a condition of taking office they swear to uphold the laws and programs that predecessors have set in place (Rose, 1990a). As long as inherited programs are deemed satisfactory, policymakers have no stimulus to search for new measures. Even if dissatisfaction occurs, new programs cannot be constructed on green field sites. Instead, they must be introduced into a policy environment dense with past commitments.

The past has two faces: history-as-continuity and history-as-intelligence (Nailor, 1991: 44n). The continuity of history is often a constraint. The continuance into the present of programs launched decades or generations ago preempts the scope for choice. Given a choice, President Reagan would not have wanted to commit hundreds of billions of dollars to Social Security and Medicare. Yet inherited legislation bound the Reagan administration to continue heavy spending on social benefits.

History as intelligence seeks to make use of experience from past times and places. There is no direct causal connection between NATO and the military alliance problems of Greek city-states 2500 years ago. Yet the founders of NATO were familiar with a lesson that Thucydides taught, namely, the importance of collective security. History as intelligence offers a wide choice of lessons that may apply in the present.

Ignorance of the past can affect policymaking, because those who do not learn lessons from mistakes of the past may be condemned to repeat them. As the military historian Michael Howard (1991) remarks:

> Our awareness of the world and our capacity to deal intelligently with its problems are shaped not only by the history we know but by what we do *not* know. Ignorance, especially the ignorance of educated men, can be a more powerful force than knowledge.

Although (or because) it is near at hand, politicians avoid examining the record of their immediate predecessors. Often it is a record of failure and a reminder that, sooner or later, they too are likely to fail. The first section of this chapter considers obstacles to searching the past: a lack of interest by policymakers and difficulties in finding applicable lessons. The second section shows what happens when policymakers do attempt to learn from their own past. They may mislead themselves by the use of dubious analogies or rely on inherited programs to provide remedies in the present. When structural changes introduce discontinuities between past and present, policymakers must turn to the future. However, knowledge about the future is speculative. Astronomers who deal with physically determined processes may confidently predict future movements in the solar system, but social scientists can only indicate probabilities of success or failure. The absence of certainty gives self-interested politicians the opportunity to make their proposals for the future a matter of unbounded faith and political will.

Obstacles to Searching the Past

The supply of history is inexhaustible, but the demand is strictly limited. First, it is limited by a shortage of time. Because policymakers are always under pressure, they have no time to study history for its own sake. Policymakers are instrumentally oriented; they seek lessons that can be used in dealing with current problems.

The vastness of the historical past is a second obstacle to its current use. The record of government action in a particular policy area fills drawer after drawer of filing cabinets. The materials are filed unselectively without a "bottom line" of lessons. When records are reported by historians, the result is usually an account of what happened in the past without specific guidance to problems here and now.

REASONS FOR LOW POLITICAL DEMAND

Policymakers have an extremely short time horizon; they live in the present. A media-oriented politician will define the present as the next deadline of a TV program or newspaper. A high-ranking agency official will see the present as the time available to prepare for tomorrow or next week's meetings. Politicians concentrate on what can be done in the span of time that is meaningful to them, the period between the last election and the next one.

The future is important to policymakers, for it appears open. Actions taken today can affect what happens tomorrow. Thus, next year's budget is deemed more important than the money spent last year, and winning the next election is an even more immediate concern to politicians than past success, which tends to be taken for granted.

Policymakers, and particularly elected politicians, usually have little or no knowledge of the history of the programs for which they are responsible. Even a degree in history is of little use, for it concentrates on the broad outlines of national and world history; it rarely goes into the detailed history of programs. The average presidential appointee has little firsthand knowledge of past government commitments to draw on. Members of Congress and their staffs, by long service on a committee, can accumulate detailed knowledge, but this is viewed instrumentally. The past is searched selectively for examples that bolster arguments for a preferred course of action in the present. The result is: "Policymakers often use history badly" (May, 1973: xi).

Politicians enter office full of confidence, for they have just won an election or won the confidence of the president who has appointed them. They see themselves as new brooms, ready to

Searching across Time

sweep away the mistakes of the past and giving fresh direction to programs for which they become responsible. Anything that happened before the last election may be dismissed as part of the antediluvian past. Often, it is a record of commitments by political opponents.

In recent years a new breed of policymaker has emerged, the ideologue committed to "timeless" truths and principles. Reaganauts and Thatcherites proclaimed principles of the market considered applicable at all times and places, especially in the administration they served. The most committed New Right supporters of President Reagan and of Margaret Thatcher did not want to learn the whys and wherefores of the programs that their predecessors had adopted. Inherited commitments were rejected as basically wrong. Their principles gave clear prescriptions about what ought to be done, and New Right ideologues saw their task as putting these principles into effect to clean up the "mess" inherited from the past. Explanations that past commitments could not easily be escaped were dismissed on principle, and anyone offering cautions based on past experience was viewed as a political opponent.

TECHNICAL OBSTACLES TO FINDING WHAT IS SOUGHT

The immediate technical obstacles to drawing lessons from the past are the large quantity of raw material available and the difficulty of refining it into the succinct lessons and gems of wisdom that policymakers seek.

The Freedom of Information Act gives everyone in Washington—policymakers, journalists, and advocates of causes—access to tons of paper and tens of thousands of shelved documents about every major public agency's programs. But just as a full mailbox is likely to be stuffed with junk mail, so official records are often "junk" documents containing tedious bureaucratic minutiae of little consequence at the time and of no long-term significance.

Assembling and analyzing the record of a program is a time-consuming and laborious task, requiring the skills of a professional historian or archivist. It is not a task that an administrator or a special assistant can undertake. Even less is it possible for a presidential appointee to spend days in a government archive trying to tease out of the record what was done wrong by predecessors.

In theory, official historians could be appointed to produce accounts that distill points of continuing relevance. In response to the stimulus of war, British governments have commissioned multivolume official histories written by specialists. One difficulty is that official histories, even though only circulating within departments, tend to have many revealing insights removed because of potential embarrassment: "They have to be officially laundered" (Nailor, 1991: 24). The use of academic historians to write accounts can produce greater detachment and objectivity, but this encourages history that emphasizes the uniqueness of past events rather than the more instrumentally oriented drawing of lessons for current policymakers.

The multimedia revolution makes it even more difficult to put together records of the recent past. Public officials no longer spend a lot of time communicating on paper, and after-the-fact notes of discussions or telephone conversations can be partial and omit much of importance. Many decisions emerge out of group discussions that wander in many directions at once. The White House tapes published as a consequence of the Watergate investigation showed that, whether President Nixon or his top advisers were discussing the cover-up of a criminal investigation, national security matters, or problems of the economy, White House discussion could be banal and lacking in analytic rigor.

In the era in which government departments were full of officials who had spent a working lifetime there, it was possible to supplement the written record by asking questions of officials involved in past events. The institutional memory of an organization was embodied in officials with many years of experience there. Today, it is an exceptional agency with many veteran officials involved in policymaking. Even more unusual is a demand from short-term political appointees to talk to those who know the history of a program that currently causes dissatisfaction. Washington is now "a government of strangers," in which layers of short-term appointees directing agencies tend to isolate themselves from those who know its history best (cf. Heclo, 1977).

Searching across Time

The value of history is greatest in government agencies bound by precedent. Every bureaucratic organization is required by law to act equitably, that is, to treat identical cases in the same way, and to treat similar cases similarly. A complex problem can sometimes be dealt with by treating some elements by precedent; for example, even if every military engagement is unique in its configuration of events, many military operations can be run by rule and precedent. In agencies that deal with a large number of welfare claimants, considerable attention is paid to recording precedents in dealing with cases.

Determining which precedent fits the facts of a particular case can easily be disputed. In the courts, precedents are important, but the facts of a case are always ambiguous. Lawyers for the plaintiff and lawyers for the defendant cite opposing precedents in favor of their clients.

Attempts to distill lessons from the past face two ineluctable problems. Any sequence of events can be subject to more than one interpretation. Historical journals are full of debates between professional historians about interpretations of the past. The greater the emphasis on examining the past for relevance to the present, the more contestable the conclusions are likely to be. Second, the lessons that policymakers want from the past depend on the situation. At one point in time officials may want to know why a program was adopted; at another point they may want to know why it was not abolished.

When policymakers are confronted with unprecedented problems, the obstacles to learning from the past are insuperable, because nothing in their own past is like the problem at hand. AIDS is an example of an unprecedented policy problem. It caught public health authorities as well as the medical profession by surprise. Because of the epidemic potential of AIDS, policymakers faced demands to do something about it. There were no established programs dealing with AIDS, nationally or in other countries. Nor was there any recognized precedent. Policymakers have thus had to reason speculatively or invoke loose analogies with public health problems from the past (Day and Klein, 1989; cf. Neustadt and Fineberg, 1983).

Learning from One's Own Past

Policymaking by routine carries reliance on the past to an extreme. In the absence of dissatisfaction, it is assumed that there is nothing to be learned in the present because what worked before is still effective. However, when routine activities do not maintain satisfaction, then policymakers must start searching, and an agency's own past is nearest at hand.

The means of searching the past are multiple. When a crisis arises, policymakers can use analogies for guidance or endorsement of present actions. When difficulties are interpreted as a consequence of a program being short of resources, then the prescription is for an incremental change: Do more of the same. If the problem is cyclical, such as an economic recession, then a remedy that worked before at a similar stage in a business cycle can be invoked again. Whereas analogies are an attempt to use history as intelligence, incremental increases and cyclical programs rely on continuity.

ANALOGIES WITH THE PAST

Drawing analogies is very different from seeking historical understanding for its own sake. A historian looks for a more or less unique configuration of circumstances that caused and resolved a situation. From the historian's perspective, the only lesson we can learn from history is that we cannot learn from history, because every event is unique. When asked to draw a lesson from the past, professional historians are usually handicapped by an excess of knowledge.

Analogies are simple. The object is to draw a lesson of immediate relevance to current needs. Reasoning by analogy requires that a past situation have similarities with a present problem of policymakers. An analogy can be based on a single point of correspondence between present and past. Given X in both past and present situations, if A was the effective response in the past, then A can be invoked again. It is not necessary to undertake a complex analysis of why the program worked in the past or to consider dissimilarities between past and present.

Reasoning by analogy is useful in communicating within an

organization. Once a current difficulty is classified as similar to a past difficulty, then everyone familiar with it will understand how to respond. Without further analysis, officials can routinely apply standard operating procedures used in the past to a problem that has been made familiar by analogy.

Reasoning by analogy appeals to politicians because it condenses much information into a few readily understood symbols. The complex procedures necessary for proper lesson-drawing, such as the construction of analytic cause-and-effect models and a prospective evaluation of consequences, are unnecessary. Policymakers can use analogies to jump to conclusions. Furthermore, policymakers can arrive at their conclusions first, and then invoke analogies as symbols to mobilize support. In short, the "uses" of history are often misuses.

Because any complex situation can have similarities with a variety of past events, it is often unclear which analogy with the past should be invoked. The debate about the Gulf war illustrates the ambiguity of history. Following the Iraqi invasion of Kuwait and before U.S. forces went into action against Saddam Hussein, General Alexander Haig (1990), a former national security assistant in the White House and NATO commander, puzzled aloud about the choice between analogies.

> International conflicts attract historical analogies the way honey attracts bears, because the "lessons learned" from such analogies are supposed to help us avoid repeating past mistakes. The Persian Gulf crisis is no exception, and two analogies in particular—Munich and Vietnam—might have something to tell us.
>
> The first, more familiar to older Americans, is Munich—the story of the disastrous appeasement of Hitler, redeemed later only by horrible loss of life in a terrible war. The second, more familiar to younger Americans, is Vietnam—the story of disastrous American military involvement, never redeemed despite its costs.
>
> Which analogy, Munich or Vietnam, the 1930s or the 1960s, has more to tell us?

Because analogies are very selective, any lesson drawn can be disputed. Haig's interpretation of Hussein as an aggressor who should not be appeased (the Munich analogy) was not the only interpretation. In the critical vote on whether to authorize military action against Iraq, almost half the Senate, bearing in mind the analogy of Vietnam, voted against military action.

Although analogies with the past are appealing, they have several analytic weaknesses. First, there are problems in searching the past to identify which situations are analogous; the more complex the problem, the more arguable the choice.

Second, there is a difficulty in discriminating between what is recurrent and what is unique in the problem at hand. Neustadt and May (1986: 235) caution policymakers considering an analogy with the past: "Quickly jotting down the *Likenesses* and *Differences* can block use of potentially misleading analogies." Third, it is usually moot whether similarities between problems at different points in time are sufficient to justify the conclusion that both will be amenable to the same solution.

The fundamental problem of analogies is that historical details are ignored; instead, it is assumed that *all* other conditions remain equal between past and present. But this ceteris paribus condition usually fails to hold, particularly in a foreign policy crisis, when analogies are often invoked. Crises are relatively infrequent and occur in very different parts of the globe. It is doubtful whether conditions remain constant between America in the 1960s and the 1990s, and even more tenuous are analogies between Europe in the 1930s and the Middle East in the 1990s.

MORE OF THE SAME

In domestic policy, continuities in programs from one year to the next are substantial, and all other conditions do tend to remain equal. When these conditions are met, policymakers can minimize search by trying to make marginal incremental changes in a program (Braybrooke and Lindblom, 1963).

When the cause of dissatisfaction is diagnosed as an inadequate commitment of resources to an established program, a response can be: Provide more of the same. If many elderly people are living in poverty, then increase social security benefits. If the education of children is causing dissatisfaction, hire more teachers and pay teachers more. If a nation's defense is the cause of anxiety, build more planes and ships and recruit more soldiers. Dissatisfaction is expected to be dissipated by the simple device of spending more money.

Doing more of the same is the simplest form of change. It takes an established program for granted; the institutions and officials responsible for implementing it remain in place, and most of its beneficiaries remain the same. There are none of the uncertainties or delays arising from the introduction of a new program. Administratively, all that is required is an alteration in the computer codes specifying the sums to be paid pensioners or teachers. Increasing a program's budget is likely to be popular with the agency responsible for it, since the agency knows how it works and does not need to implement a new measure. Spending more money will be welcomed by the clients of a program, too.

Responding with more of the same assumes that no fresh lesson can be learned from signals of dissatisfaction; all that is necessary is to believe that more is better. The causal mechanisms that have produced satisfaction in the past are assumed to remain effective. It is also assumed that the ratio of output to input is constant, so that allocating more money to an established program will produce more satisfaction rather than increase inefficiency. No allowance is made for the possibility that the policy environment has so changed that more of the same will not be good enough.

THE SAME AS BEFORE

Recurring patterns of fluctuation in the policy environment create cyclical problems. In such circumstances, persistence in a given policy or spending more will not remove dissatisfaction. For example, a big increase in unemployment in the wake of rising interest rates will be exacerbated rather than removed by still higher interest rates. To stop dissatisfaction, something different must be done.

When problems are cyclical, their recurrence can be met by invoking a familiar program that has brought satisfaction before. For example, Keynesian prescriptions for managing the economy assume both upswings and downturns in the economy and prescribe policy responses for each reversal in the cycle. Rising unemployment can be met by boosting demand through increasing public expenditure or cutting taxes; a rise in the rate of inflation can be met by reducing spending or raising taxes.

Invoking a cyclical program in response to a cyclical problem requires the minimum of search in the past. Officials know that they can implement a cyclical measure because they have used it before. Nor does it require examining experience elsewhere. The speed of response is much greater than for a novel program. Critics can be silenced with the statement that the program being invoked has already demonstrated its effectiveness.

The impact of a cyclical program is expected to be the same as before, as no long-term change is thought to have occurred in the policy environment. The departure from a satisfactory equilibrium is diagnosed as temporary and familiar; invoking a familiar program promises a return to the previous equilibrium.

When the past is a record of mistakes, negative lessons can be drawn by policymakers averse to repeating past mistakes. Their decision rule is to do something different than before. The defense policies of Germany and Japan today represent lessons learned about what not to do. For the first half of the twentieth century, each country pursued an aggressive policy of military conquest; these policies ended in disaster in 1945. The conclusion drawn was that military expansion could lead to disaster, for their own country as well as others. In reaction, both Germany and Japan have placed in their constitutions an explicit prohibition against the aggressive deployment of military force.

A TIME FOR DISCONTINUITIES

Drawing lessons from the past assumes great continuity between the more or less recent past and the present. In the short term, an assumption of continuity is usually justified. But in the long term this is often not the case.

Short-term incremental changes rely on continuity between the past and present. In any given year, adding a small amount to the base of program expenditure produces a marginal change. More than a quarter century ago Braybrooke and Lindblom (1963:

99f) described social security legislation as an example of incrementalism "since it is amended every few years to increase incrementally the level of benefits."

However, because each annual increment is added to an already substantial base, incremental changes compound. Incremental changes have expanded social security expenditures in three major ways: The value of the benefit paid each individual has increased; eligibility for social security benefits has been broadened so that today nearly everyone in the labor force becomes eligible for benefits; and the total number of persons of retirement age has increased.

Compounding generates a cumulative impact magnitudes greater than relatively small annual rates of change. When Braybrooke and Lindblom published their comments in 1963, the total cash payment from the Social Security System was $14.5 billion. The effect of compounding the above changes is that in 1992 the cash cost is $284 billion. Today's policymakers have inherited social security programs that are a source of budgetary dissatisfaction because of the cumulative effect of compounding.

Compounding can create discontinuities as a consequence of the slow but steady effects of annual changes. In a classic study of the federal budget, Dempster and Wildavsky (1979) argued that budgeting was incremental because changes in program expenditures tended to be regular from one year to the next. The size of the change, which varied from program to program, was said to be less significant than regularity in the annual rate of change.

Because each year's change is added to the one that went before, in the fullness of time seemingly small changes can add up to big totals. The Dempster and Wildavsky study found that the median change in spending on domestic programs over the previous twenty-five years had been 6.8 percent a year. Yet compounding this rate over two and one-half decades transforms its scale. A growth rate of 6.8 percent a year doubles expenditure in a decade, trebles costs in sixteen years, and more than quadruples expenditure in a quarter century. One-quarter of programs saw their expenditure grow by at least 17.8 percent a year, and one-quarter had a negative annual growth rate or a growth rate of zero. Compounding each of these three representative rates of growth results not only in a transformation in the absolute size of the great majority of programs but also a transformation in the relationship between those that are relatively large and small.

Discontinuities can also result from changes in the policy environment. For generations policymakers in the Deep South were committed to programs of racial segregation. When federal courts ordered change, the first response of all-white state governments was to invoke subterfuges that had worked before. When civil rights protesters took to the streets in unprecedented nonviolent protests, local police and vigilantes responded as before, that is, with violence. However, changes in the policy environment between the 1930s, when efforts to end segregation could be evaded or repressed, and the 1960s created a discontinuity. Race relations in the South could no longer be controlled by policies of "more of the same" and "the same as before."

In the fullness of time, continuity is eroded. Structural changes in the policy environment, including the cumulative compounding of established programs, sooner or later introduce structural discontinuities. The result is that programs that have brought satisfaction in the past become identified as a cause of dissatisfaction, and policymakers must search farther afield.

Unbounded Speculation about the Future

When the past is characterized by failure and the present by dissatisfaction, policymakers can turn to speculation about the future. The goal is removing dissatisfaction, but the means to this end are uncertain. By definition the future cannot be known, and there are many different ways to remove dissatisfaction. Because proposals for future action are likely to be disputed, no consensus is likely about the bounds of speculation. A proposal that appears desirable and reasonable to one group will appear out of bounds to another.

Although policymakers cannot draw lessons from events that have yet to occur, they can try to anticipate events. In doing so, they may treat the future as an extension of the present in order to bound speculation by existing knowledge. Theorists can claim future success for their prescriptions on the grounds that predictions follow logically from premises, whether or not their premises are plausible. Politicians can exploit uncertainty about the future by willfully asserting faith in their proposals, which have yet to be proven wrong.

ANTICIPATING DIFFICULTIES IN IMPLEMENTATION

The adoption of a new program is intended to remove dissatisfaction, but its very novelty creates uncertainties. Care in implementation seeks to fill the gap between a decision being made and a program going into effect.

Planning to implement a new program is speculative, insofar as it involves "If ..., then ..." hypotheses about how a new program is expected to work. Even though a program may be novel in its goal, many elements are likely to involve standard operating procedures. This is the case with bureaucratic rules and regulations, accountability to superiors and the courts, and the pay and recruitment of personnel. Insofar as a new program is akin to another program, experienced administrators can draw on their past experience to incorporate tested procedures in plans for implementation.

The less the difference between a "new" program and established programs, the higher the probability that it can be implemented. However, the less the change involved in such a program, the greater the risk that it will not be sufficient to dispel high levels of dissatisfaction.

The strength of implementation analysis is also its weakness. Focusing on what administrators can and cannot do stresses the need for realizable programs to achieve rhetorical goals of politicians. But the approach is a weakness insofar as it redirects a search away from innovation to familiar and easily implemented programs. The greater the dissatisfaction with the present, the less policymakers are likely to accept procedures that are closely related to programs identified as unsatisfactory. There will be openness to programs based on speculation unbounded by the past.

ATTRACTIONS OF SCIENTISM

New programs are necessarily speculative. In a scientific setting speculative reasoning is familiar. Theoretical models are constructed that explain important phenomena in clear and logical terms without regard to their application in problem-solving contexts. The actual implementation of the blueprints—building a bridge or a jet plane—may involve many practical difficulties, yet as long as all the steps in the chain of reasoning have been correctly specified, the bridge should stand and the plane ought to fly.

Scientism assumes that the logic and methods of the natural sciences can be transferred to the social sciences. The construction of a mathematical model that "solves" a problem in the abstract depends on the following simplifying assumptions: (1) All the critical determinants of an outcome have been identified. (2) All the critical variables can be quantified and relationships between them stated with precision. (3) Cause-and-effect relations are the same in the future as in the past. (4) The omission of institutional and contextual factors included in cause-and-effect models of prospective evaluation is of no consequence. When these conditions are met, the uncertainties of future speculation may be replaced with mechanical certainties.

Confining a model to quantifiable elements makes it possible for outcomes to be predictable—but only within the terms of the model. Numbers can be produced to represent how many people are affected, the amount of money budgeted, and the probability of a given measure achieving a given effect—assuming that the model is an accurate representation of reality. The results are reduced to a positive or negative ratio of costs to benefits. However, a cost-benefit ratio is only an estimate of what would result if someone else figured out how to put the program into effect.

Although logic can be a powerful analytic tool, it sometimes produces results that are, in the English locution, "too clever by half." In public policy, the usefulness of a model does not depend on its logical clarity but on its applicability.

The workings of public programs are fundamentally different from the certainties associated with scientific phenomena. No social science theory identifies all the influences that determine the outcomes of a public program. Nor is it possible to quantify all the significant determinants of outcomes; public programs are subject to qualitative as well as quantitative influences.

The use of quantified forecasting models to test whether programs will work is particularly suspect when dissatisfaction is caused by structural change. The validity of statistical models depends on the assumption that past relations of cause and effect will continue in the future. However, when past remedies fail to remove present dissatisfaction, it is more reasonable to assume that statistical data from the past will not be a realistic guide to the future.

UNBOUNDED FAITH AND WILL

Uncertainties about the future allow policymakers to slip the bounds of evidence. If they so wish, policymakers can evaluate the likely impact of a program in terms of unbounded faith, believing whatever they would like to believe, or arguing whatever they would like others to believe. Statements about the future consequences of present proposals then become a battle of political wills.

A tactically shrewd politician can exploit uncertainty about the future. If a program is disliked, a politician can oppose it on the grounds that success is not certain. If a program is considered desirable, a politician can advocate it on the grounds that it cannot be described as unworkable. The absence of certainty is interpreted as showing that there is no proof that a proposal will not work.

Politicians can welcome freedom from constraint when making promises about the future. Speculating about the future has a visionary appeal. It is possible to express values and affirm ideals above and beyond immediate concerns. The immediate stimulus of dissatisfaction can be used as an opportunity to urge how the world ought to be remade.

When prescriptions about the future are derived from values not subject to any empirical constraints, then faith can become the ground for acceptance. When a goal is deemed desirable, faith can be used to justify the belief that a proposal will succeed. The absence of certainty is used to obliterate the distinction between what is desirable and what is possible.

Politicians can use the authority of office to enforce faith. Discussions can focus on the ideological values on which a program is based, rather than on the mechanisms by which it is expected to become effective. A skeptic asking why it is believed that a program will work can be told: You have to believe. Refusal to believe can be interpreted as a rejection of core values of the government of the day and can lead to an individual being excluded from the policymaking process.

Margaret Thatcher's insistence on the introduction of a poll tax to raise revenue for British local government illustrates how a strong will can impose a program based on highly speculative assumptions. Faced with dissatisfaction about local property taxes that were effective but unpopular, Mrs. Thatcher chose on a priori grounds to replace it with a flat-rate poll tax on every adult. The proposal attracted much criticism on practical and normative grounds. Since a poll tax is not used to finance local government in any other advanced industrial nation, the prime minister could dismiss such criticisms as purely speculative.

Although Margaret Thatcher had the will to introduce a novel tax, her will could not control the outcome. The introduction of the poll tax stimulated much dissatisfaction among both supporters and partisan opponents. Tax rates were much higher than anticipated and implementation was far more difficult than assumed; the result was a large shortfall in revenue. Dissatisfaction stimulated sharp attacks from Conservatives who had previously avoided challenging the prime minister's will. Within a year Thatcher had lost office by a vote of her former supporters in Parliament, and her successor, John Major, announced the abandonment of the unsuccessful innovation.

When the past is associated with failure and speculation about the future is remote from present realities, policymakers can no longer confine their search to their own past and future. They must also search for lessons across space.

5

Searching across Space

Humani nil a me alienum puto.
(Nothing that concerns man is alien to me.)

— Terence, c. 160 B.C.

*I*solation has never been possible in the world of politics. In classical Greece, Athenians studied neighboring city-states in order to draw lessons from their allies and enemies. The Founding Fathers were separated from Europe by a voyage of many weeks; nonetheless, they studied what was done there in order to learn lessons from the mistakes of foreign monarchs. Today, nations as remote as Nepal are members of the International Monetary Fund, and Berkeley-trained students can be found in ministries of finance from Katmandu to Stockholm.

Yet many theories of public policy imply autarky, that is, self-sufficiency in making decisions. Little allowance is made for decisions within a political system being influenced by what happens outside it. The structure and process of a given system—its political values and institutions, party competition, socioeconomic characteristics, et cetera—are assumed to be the only influences that determine domestic policy outcomes. What happens outside its boundaries is ignored completely.

Studies of comparative public policy typically examine systems in parallel, arraying countries separately for examination of similarities and differences. It is assumed that countries, like parallel lines, never meet. Similarities are explained as a consequence of common influences within each system producing similar effects; a country with a social democratic government and a high standard of living is expected to adopt welfare-state programs in response to domestic pressures and to do so without examining experience abroad (cf. Rose, 1991a: 453ff).

Lesson-drawing does not deny that lines on maps separate the territorial responsibilities of government, but it also emphasizes interaction between parallel agencies. Even though cities, states, or nations do not merge, common problems create common interests in public policy, and if agencies respond differently, the potential for lesson-drawing exists.

When policymakers search for lessons across space, three influences direct attention. *Money* matters, for programs vary greatly in what they cost, and it is hard to apply lessons learned from programs beyond the fiscal means of a public agency. Within a country, differences in per capita income are limited, but total public revenue differs greatly. A suburb may have a higher per capita income than a big city, but its total tax base is not big enough to finance the cultural, sporting, and educational facilities of a big city. The same is true of countries; small countries as rich as Denmark or Norway lack the aggregate resources to finance space exploration or defense programs on the scale that the United States can support.

Geographical propinquity influences where policymakers look for lessons. A nearby government is the easiest place to look—assuming that its resources are also similar. Every town hall and state house has a multiplicity of neighbors to turn to for ideas. Most national governments also have many neighbors. The United States is unusual in being a continental country with only two neighbors, Canada and Mexico. By contrast, a European country such as France has seven neighbors, and Germany has eight.

Ideological propinquity matters too, for policymakers will only introduce programs consistent with their own values. Hence, Democratic governors may look to other states with liberal programs, and Republican governors to states with conservative programs. Internationally, social democrats tend to believe that they have more to learn from other social democratic governments, and conservatives look to free-market administrations elsewhere for lessons. A few states may be considered exemplars, and distance can even add attractions. For more than a century Japan has sought lessons from America and Europe rather than from Asia, Europeans have looked to America rather than to such neighbors as Turkey, and Americans have looked to Europe rather than to Mexico.

As long as there is incompatibility between aspirations and achievements, there is motive to search across space. Searching is easiest within a nation, the subject of the first section of this chapter. State and local officials do not need a passport to see how other governments handle a common problem, and within-nation differences in resources, distances, and values tend to be limited. National policymakers often have problems like those of other countries rather than those of mayors and governors; hence, the second section examines searching in an increasingly permeable international system. Since lesson-drawing concerns both time and space, the conclusion shows how the search for lessons can bridge the present and future. East European governments that see themselves as backward can strive to catch up, and policymakers in advanced industrial nations can use prospective evaluation to analyze whether programs effective elsewhere would work here in the future.

Searching within a National System

The easiest place to search for lessons is within one's own country, for preconditions for lesson-drawing are easily met. There cannot be a total blockage on the transfer of programs between cities and states when Congress and the Supreme Court have the authority to encourage or compel the diffusion of a program nationwide.

The fifty states of America are both diverse and numerous; they are three times the number of the sixteen *länder* in a united Germany, five times the number of Canadian provinces, and more than eight times as numerous as the federal states of Australia. The number and diversity of states, however, can be an argument against indiscriminate lesson-drawing. A program suitable for

Alaska or Rhode Island can be unsuited for California or New York. Lesson-drawing is not about the uniform spread of programs throughout a nation; it is about finding programs that can transfer.

SIMILARITY OF ECONOMIC RESOURCES

Economic conditions are often cited as a prime determinant of public policy. The starting point is a simple proposition that there is a minimum threshold of cost for any given program. While many Third World countries cannot afford programs found in the United States or Western Europe, there is no such barrier to lesson-drawing within the United States. Income differences between states can influence the level at which a program is funded, but rarely do they preclude adoption.

Although American states differ in per capita income, they do not differ greatly. In 1990 personal income per capita was $18,685 nationwide. Two-thirds of the states had an income that was at least 90 percent of this average. Even the poorest states, Mississippi and West Virginia, had a higher average income than such OECD countries as New Zealand, Spain, and Ireland.

Differences in income between states are decreasing. In 1990 only two states had an income more than a quarter below the national average. By contrast, in 1964 eight states did; and at the end of the 1920s boom, eighteen states were more than a quarter below the national average income (ACIR, 1987: 110; 1991, 33).

Fiscal equalization programs facilitate lesson-drawing by transferring money between jurisdictions in order to reduce inequalities in resources. Within a state, fiscal equalization programs fund many programs of poorer communities, such as education. The federal government annually appropriates tens of billions for equalization programs, thereby redistributing income from richer states and cities to poorer states, principally in the South and West (Wright, 1990). A condition of state and federal categoric grants is that the recipients adopt specific programs. Thus, grants to poorer areas stimulate their recipients to search for programs to meet state and federal funding standards (Berry and Berry, 1990: 396; Savage, 1985: 14).

Differences between states in tax revenue reflect political choice as well as state income. Tax effort—that is, the percentage of personal income collected in state and local taxes—varies greatly within the United States. The median state collects 11 percent of personal income in state and local taxes. However, Arkansas collects 21 percent of personal income in tax and New York 16 percent. By contrast, New Hampshire collects only 8 percent in tax, and Missouri 9 percent (ACIR, 1991: 247).

Differences in tax effort are not directly determined by differences in state income. Connecticut and Illinois rank well above average in per capita income but are among the bottom five states in tax effort, each collecting less than 14 percent of personal income in state and local taxes. States can be below average in income and yet levy relatively high taxes. North Dakota collects an average of 20 percent of income in taxes, and Louisiana collects the equivalent of 19 percent of income in state and local taxes.

Structural inequalities within states constitute the chief veto on lesson-drawing. Big cities have very large tax bases because they combine industrial and commercial activities with large populations. For example, a city such as Chicago can command resources that no other city in Illinois can match, and Atlanta has resources different in kind from any other city in Georgia. Wealthy suburbs have tax bases different in kind from poor suburbs, small towns, and rural counties.

GEOGRAPHICAL PROPINQUITY

Neighbors are a convenient source of ideas. A local government official is usually within a local telephone call or an hour's drive of opposite numbers in a similar office. The viewership of local television stations and the readership of newspapers often cover dozens of different government jurisdictions. However, nearness does not guarantee similarities in resources or political outlooks. Within a metropolitan area, a big city mayor sees urban problems very differently than a suburban city manager. Within a state, rural counties often consider urban programs irrelevant to their concerns just as urban counties find rural programs irrelevant.

Geography can draw together policymakers in different jurisdictions. When a state capital is located in the center of a state, many cities and counties will be closer to other states than to their own legislature. New York City, for example, is wedged between Connecticut and New Jersey; relative to Albany, it is out on a limb.

Interstate compacts are a striking example of officials in different jurisdictions agreeing on programs to deal with a problem of common interest, such as the Delaware River Basin compact, involving Delaware, New Jersey, New York, Pennsylvania, and the federal government. The growth of compacts in the postwar era reflects an increased tendency of state and local governments to look at programs across state lines (Council of State Governments, 1990: 565ff).

Geography can also draw cities and states together across international boundaries. Fourteen American states share a boundary with Canada, and four with Mexico. Florida is closer to Cuba than to Washington, D.C., Texas is closer to Mexico, and Hawaii is closer to Japan. Alaska is closer to Siberia than to any other American state.

In a country as vast as the United States, "nearness" is relative. It can refer to states that are geographically contiguous or to regions, such as the South or the West, in which state capitals can be up to a thousand miles apart (Berry and Berry, 1990: 406; Walker, 1969: 891ff).

Because every government shares boundaries with a number of neighbors, policymakers must choose which neighbors are "nearest" in a given policy area and which to ignore. A border state such as Missouri can choose whether to see itself as part of the industrial Midwest, since it borders Illinois; of the South, since it borders Arkansas, Kentucky, and Tennessee; or of the Plains region, since it borders Kansas and Iowa. In income terms, Missouri appears closer to Illinois than to Arkansas, but in spending on education Missouri looks south to low-spending states.

Among a group of more or less like-minded states, one or two can be regarded as exemplars, whose programs constitute the best practice that other states may emulate. In the Progressive era, a small number of states pioneered new programs. A 1912 tribute to Wisconsin declared:

Searching across Space

Wisconsin is doing for America what Germany is doing for the world. It is an experiment station in politics, in social and industrial legislation, in the democratization of science and higher education. It is a state-wide laboratory in which popular government is being tested. (Quoted in Clemens, 1990: 19)

Surveys find that California, Minnesota, and Massachusetts are the three states most frequently regarded as leaders in developing new programs that may be adapted elsewhere. Michigan, New Jersey, New York, Florida, and Iowa rank next (cf. Council on State Governments, 1990: 394; Grupp and Richards, 1975: 853; Savage, 1978).

Expert officials define propinquity in terms of similarity in professional interests (table 5.1). When asked what their best sources of information are, first place is given to informal contacts with others in their own agency and related state offices. Second in

TABLE 5.1
INFORMATION SOURCES OF INNOVATIVE
STATE OFFICIALS

	USEFULNESS[a]
Informal communication in agency	6.1
Informal communication with other state workers	5.4
Professional association publications	5.4
Professional meetings	5.2
Informal communication with colleagues in other states	4.8
Interest groups	4.7
Citizens	4.7
News media	4.6
Academic research and reports	4.5
Federal government	4.4

SOURCE: Source: Grady and Chi (1990: table 1), survey of state government officials responsible for programs nominated for Council of State Governments' Innovations Transfer Program.

a. Maximum value = 7.

importance are formal professional networks joining like-minded officials across state lines. Some conventional sources of new ideas, such as the news media, academic research, and the federal government, come at the bottom of the list (see also Klingman, 1980).

IDEOLOGICAL NEARNESS

Like-mindedness in political values is a key element in choosing friends and neighbors to turn to. This is rational, for lessons can only be chosen in relation to political goals. Politicians may not know how to design a new program, but they can indicate clearly what lessons they would veto as unacceptable to their political values and interests. Non-elected officials cannot ignore this; they look to their governor and legislators for cues about political goals (Brudney and Hebert, 1987: 193; see also Sabatier and Whiteman, 1985).

We would expect states dominated by the Republican party or by conservative Democrats to look for ideas to other states with similar governments, and states dominated by liberal Democrats to look to other liberal states. Partisan values are specially likely to influence lesson-drawing on left-right economic issues. Even though every state legislature is familiar with both pro-business and pro-union programs, a state is not likely to adopt programs favoring conflicting interests. A liberal state would be expected to adopt liberal labor and welfare programs, and a conservative state to favor pro-business programs. The importance of partisanship is often overlooked in technocratically biased studies of policy diffusion and in studies about programs such as state lotteries, which are not easily linked to left-right differences.

A review of six labor and welfare programs found that forty of the forty-eight continental states consistently favor programs of the left or right, endorsing either liberal or conservative labor, welfare, and wage programs dealing with right to work, mandatory plant closing prenotification, extended AFDC eligibility and so forth (figure 5.1). Eighteen northern-tier states from California through Minnesota to Massachusetts consistently adopt liberal measures. They are complemented by twenty-two southern-tier states only interested in lessons consistent with right-wing values;

Searching across Space

	CONSERVATIVE PROGRAMS	
	ENACTED	NOT ENACTED
LIBERAL PROGRAMS — ENACTED	Inconsistent: 7 IA, KS, MO, MI, NE, NH, SC	Consistent: 18 CA, CT, DE, IL, MA, MD, ME, MN, MT, NJ, NY, OH, PA, RI, VT, WA, WV, WI
LIBERAL PROGRAMS — NOT ENACTED	Consistent: 22 AL, AZ, AR, CO, FL, GA, ID, IN, KY, LA, MS, NV, NC, ND, NM, OK, SD, TN, TX, UT, VA, WY	Inconsistent: 1 OR

FIGURE 5.1

CONSISTENCY IN ADOPTION OF CONSERVATIVE OR LIBERAL SOCIAL PROGRAMS

SOURCE: Robertson (1991: table 1). Liberal laws: mandatory plant prenotification law, a minimum wage higher than the federal level, and extended AFDC eligibility in unemployed families. Conservative laws: right to work, repeal of prevailing wage law, or "man-in-the-house" welfare law.

this group extends from Arizona through Texas to Virginia. Only eight of forty-eight states are inconsistent in the lessons that they draw about labor and welfare programs.

Searching within a Permeable International System

While every state may claim to be sovereign, it is not impermeable, that is, insulated from everything that happens elsewhere in the world. This is true of the trade in ideas as well as in the exchange of goods and services and power and influence.

CLUSTERS OF RESOURCES

On a worldwide basis, differences between nations in resources and socioeconomic development are far greater than differences between American states or Canadian provinces. American policymakers would not expect to learn much by examining programs in poor countries. Reciprocally, policymakers in a country where the population is largely illiterate and working outside the official money economy will not be able to apply lessons learned from a trip to the United States or Sweden. The journeys to progress that Third World countries are making depend less on lessons drawn from rich societies than on lessons drawn from countries in similar conditions or learned by trial and error from their own experience (cf. Hirschman, 1958).

Countries can be clustered according to the resources that they can mobilize for public policy. The United Nations Development Program (1991: 119–21) identifies fifty-three as high in such measures as life expectancy and literacy and having a gross domestic product per capita of more than $9000. Forty-four are in the medium category, having fairly high literacy levels, life expectancy rates that match the rates of some population groups in the United States, and a median gross domestic product per capita just below $3000. The least developed sixty-three countries have a life expectancy rate under fifty years at birth, less than half their adult population literate, and a median gross domestic product per person of around $900 a year. These three principal clusters can be further refined: for example, by grouping formerly centrally planned economies dominated by the old Soviet Union and by grouping more than a dozen countries that are rich because of oil exports but often lacking other resources (cf. International Monetary Fund, 1991: 123ff).

The resources required to apply a lesson usually can be stated in thresholds; that is, a country must have more than a given level of money to adopt a program. They do not depend on relative rankings. A government does not need to be one of the dozen richest in the world to achieve national literacy; it simply needs money to pay teachers and build elementary schools.

Growth in the international economy is reducing the extent to which financial resources are a barrier to drawing lessons. Dozens of countries have raised their living standards from low to middle income or from middle income to the standard of advanced industrial nations as of 1960, the year in which OECD was founded. Newly industrializing countries are now able to adopt social programs at a lower level of economic development than those at which European nations introduced comparable programs (Collier and Messick, 1975: 1307ff).

SEARCHING THE GLOBE SELECTIVELY

When national policymakers start searching for lessons across international borders, there is no limit to the distance that can be traveled. Once policymakers go to an airport with their passports in hand, they can cross continents and oceans. That distance is no obstacle to lesson-drawing is made evident by the continuing traffic across the Atlantic between Europe and the United States.

Intergovernmental and international organizations encourage exchanges of ideas between countries with similar levels of economic resources. The European Community and OECD encourage exchanges among advanced industrial nations. The collapse of the Communist system is creating a group of more than a dozen states that may learn from each other ways to make a transition to the market economy and democracy. The IMF promotes lessons drawn from the experience of countries that have large foreign debts, and the World Bank and many United Nations agencies focus on programs of concern to developing countries.

The awareness of foreign nations and cultures is variable between nations. An unobtrusive measure of the openness to foreign contacts is a country's use of the international telephone (figure 5.2, p. 106). In a small country such as the Netherlands, on a per capita basis people are more likely to be in telephone contact with other nations than in a larger country such as West Germany. A more prosperous country such as France is more likely to have international links than Italy. The United States is distinctive because, even though Americans are intensive users of the telephone, they make far fewer international phone calls than Europeans make.

Neighbors can be enemies instead of friends; hence, geographical propinquity is a weak determinant of the direction of cross-national search. For four decades the Iron Curtain created an unbridgeable gulf between neighboring countries in Central Europe. Communist-dominated states were not allowed to consider programs by their neighbors because they were deemed inconsistent with Marxist-Leninist doctrines. Germany was an extreme example of this division, for the Bonn government looked to the West, and the Communist regime in East Berlin looked to Moscow.

	AVERAGE MINUTES PER PERSON PER YEAR
Netherlands	49
West Germany	41
Britain	31
France	29
United States	22
Italy	14

FIGURE 5.2

INTERNATIONAL TELEPHONE CALLS

SOURCE: Derived from Greg Staple, *The Global Telecommunication Traffic Boom* (London: International Institute of Communication, 1990); data for minutes of outgoing international calls in 1988.

Different parts of a nation can look to contrasting neighbors. The German Rhineland is closer to the Benelux nations than to Berlin, Bavaria borders on Austria and Czechoslovakia, and former East German lands border on Poland. Northern regions of Italy are closer to Austria, to France, or to Slovenia than to Rome, and the Italian south is closer to Greece or Albania.

The permeability of national borders is leading to "leapfrogging" in which subnational levels of government coordinate responses to common problems across international boundaries. Leapfrogging assumes that national differences in institutions are less important than the functional interdependence of problems. There are formal mechanisms for cooperation between Mexico and the states of California, Arizona, and New Mexico. Transborder "summit" meetings on matters of mutual concern are also held between governors of American states and premiers of adjacent Canadian provinces (see, e.g., Duchacek, 1984: 13ff).

Many American states now energetically pursue investment from Europe, the Far East, and other parts of the world. The search for foreign investment requires a state's policymakers to relate state programs in taxation, education, and labor legislation to programs abroad. Kincaid (1984: 101) describes leapfrogging by state governors as a logical extension of the governor's domestic role as an ambassador in intergovernmental relations.

In Europe local policymakers, too, are starting to leapfrog national capitals. Cities that believe national programs neglect their concerns can turn for ideas to similarly positioned cities elsewhere in Europe. The OECD and the European Community sponsor a local employment initiative that brings together cities with similar problems in different countries—for example, old industrial and port cities such as Hamburg and Liverpool, and geographically isolated towns outside industrial areas such as Ravenna, Italy, and Limerick, Ireland (Pellegrin, 1989).

Britain is an extreme example of policymakers ignoring geographical propinquity in favor of social psychological proximity. Ireland and France are each less than twenty-five miles from Great Britain, yet policymakers in London never think of looking there for lessons in public policy. British policymakers often look across the ocean to the United States or Canada, or even farther away to Australia.

CROSS-NATIONAL SIMILARITIES IN VALUES

A few countries stand out as exemplars, attracting a stream of visitors to examine their programs. In Europe, Sweden has long been recognized as an exemplar of a social democratic welfare state, attracting interest from many who wish their own national government would draw lessons from Swedish programs. Free-market proponents examine Sweden for faults that can be used as ammunition attacking the importation of Swedish social programs.

Germany's success in controlling inflation has led many nations to seek lessons from the German *Bundesbank* (federal central bank). The institutional structure of the German central bank is studied in the belief that its structure also accounts for its capacity to introduce and maintain anti-inflationary programs (cf. Goodman, 1991). The historic success of Germany's anti-inflation programs has given the deutsche mark the leading position among European currencies and makes it the exemplar currency for the proposed European monetary union.

The United States has been an exemplar since its foundation as the first democratic nation. The richness of the American economy has also made it attractive as a source of ideas. A British policymaker in urban affairs comments: "There is a feeling that America is a confident country, prepared to try things out. We work things out more cautiously. This doesn't necessarily mean that America always gets things right, but it does mean that we can learn from the States" (quoted in Wolman, 1990).

Japan has moved from seeking examples to being an exemplar. For a century, it was a relatively poor Asian country intent on borrowing widely from Europe and America. Its success has been so great that now other nations look to Japan for ideas. The so-called Four Little Dragons of South Korea, Taiwan, Hong Kong, and Singapore have immediate economic inducements to do so, and Singapore and Malaysia have officially adopted Learning from Japan programs (cf. Westney, 1987; Shapiro, 1988; Amsden, 1990).

The attractiveness of other nations is a function of the political values of the searching nation as well as of programs in place. No one country can be an exemplar for all advanced industrial nations because countries differ in their dominant political values and in what they choose to do with their wealth. Rich nations in Scandinavia maintain big-spending social programs, whereas countries such as the United States and Japan spend much less of their national product on social programs (figure 5.3). Hence, less rich countries that do not want a big government can look to the

United States or across the Pacific to Japan, whereas countries that have or aspire to big-spending social programs can look north to Scandinavia.

Differences in political values simultaneously create divisions within nations and cross-national attractions among like-minded groups of parties. The British Conservative administrations of Margaret Thatcher and John Major found it congenial to look to the Reagan-Bush administration for programs emphasizing free

		WEALTH	
		RICHEST	LESS RICH
SIZE OF GOVERNMENT	BIG	5: Norway Sweden Germany Denmark France $13,708 [a] 51.1 [b]	5: Netherlands Italy Belgium Austria Ireland $11,102 [a] 49.5 [b]
	LESS BIG	6: United States Canada Switzerland Japan Finland Australia $15,003 [a] 34.8 [b]	5: United Kingdom New Zealand Spain Greece Portugal $8,872 [a] 40.3 [b]

FIGURE 5.3

DIFFERENCES IN VALUES AND RESOURCES
AMONG OECD NATIONS

SOURCE: Derived from OECD data reported in Rose (1991b: table 7.5).
 a. Gross domestic product per capita.
 b. Public expenditures as percentage of gross domestic product.

enterprise. By contrast, the British Labour party looks to Scandinavian and German social democratic parties.

The European Parliament institutionalizes cross-national ideological groupings, for individuals elected from twelve different nations sit together by party groups rather than dividing along national lines. International party groupings in the European Parliament include Socialists, Christian Democrats, Liberals, and Greens. The politics of the European Community reflects these divisions, in such matters as disputes about whether the Single European Market should emphasize freedom from regulation or social programs.

The incentive for policymakers to search across national boundaries is the same as the argument against doing so, namely, that programs differ. Crossing national boundaries greatly expands the number of programs that can be observed in action. The fact that they are foreign introduces an element of speculation about whether they can transfer. But speculation is bounded, for experience elsewhere provides palpable evidence of how programs actually work.

Bridging Time and Space: Their Present, Our Future

The first step in lesson-drawing is to locate a problem in time and space; drawing a lesson involves searching across both. Bridging the gap between the present and the future introduces another and more uncertain dimension. The future is not amenable to direct observation; it must be an object of speculation. Yet the future cannot be ignored in lesson-drawing. The point of searching for programs elsewhere is to find measures there that can change the future here.

Policymakers cannot let uncertainty justify inaction. When dissatisfaction with the present is high, new measures must be introduced. The bigger the push of inherited difficulties, as in East European efforts to introduce a market economy, the more difficult it is to evaluate the process as a whole. The more narrowly focused the program, such as a measure to deal with vocational education and training, the greater the likelihood of bounding speculation through a prospective evaluation that bridges the present and future.

LESSON-DRAWING AS A MEANS OF CATCHING UP

Since the industrial revolution, a few nations have always been in the lead economically; hence, for most nations economic development has been about catching up. The present achievements of a richer country are taken as an example of what a less prosperous country can achieve—if it draws appropriate lessons.

Eastern European countries today are a striking example of nations seeking to catch up, politically and economically, by drawing lessons from democratic nations with market economies. When asked whether or not their country needs development typical of Western nations, an overwhelming majority of East Europeans say that it does (figure 5.4). Lessons are sought because the great majority recognize that they do not yet have the kind of

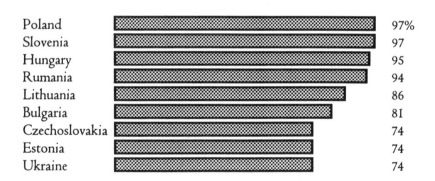

FIGURE 5.4

EAST EUROPEAN DESIRE TO LEARN FROM THE WEST (PERCENTAGE AGREEING WITH STATEMENT: "OUR COUNTRY NEEDS TO DEVELOP LIKE WESTERN NATIONS.")

SOURCE: Bruszt and Simon, (1991). Q.49.
NOTE: "Don't know"s, averaging 16 percent of respondents, omitted.

democracy that West European countries have, and they wish to achieve it.

The distance to be covered is substantial but not in principle unbridgeable. Until World War II, states such as Czechoslovakia, Poland, and Hungary were part of the European family of nations, and their levels of economic development were not different in kind from those of many neighbors. East Germany was an integral part of the German state. Even though the standard of living in East European nations today is substantially lower than in the United States, the same is true of such OECD nations as Greece, Spain, and Portugal. East European nations are not poor or backward in a Third World sense; the majority have a good secondary education and up to half of the families have a car.

The unique problem of East European governments is that they cannot draw lessons from their experience of the past four decades, because post-Communist regimes are founded on a rejection of a Soviet-style regime. Four decades of a centrally planned economy in a one-party state have left many examples of what *not* to do. Repression and inefficiency have made the old system a source of absolute dissatisfaction (Rose, 1992). Dissatisfaction produces a positive stimulus to search, but it does not tell East Europeans where to look for lessons in creating a market economy.

Pure speculation offers one source of lessons. Economic theories make very explicit the attributes of a market economy. The basic assumption of neoclassical economists is that people are everywhere the same, rationally seeking to maximize their self-interest. Introducing market mechanisms will therefore lead people to behave as in Western economies, and the dynamic of economic growth will be self-perpetuating. An expert in the area advises governments that there is no need to write new tax laws from scratch; "simply copy applicable legislation from the European Community" (Richard Portes, quoted in Khanna, 1991: 278). No prospective evaluation is required for prescriptions drawn from pure theory. It is assumed that reasoning logically from correct premises will lead to expected results. The only empirical evaluation that can be carried out is after the fact—when it will be too late if the assumptions prove incomplete and inadequate (cf. Etzioni, 1991).

Turning to other countries for lessons is another alternative. But which country or countries? It is debatable whether the richest countries of Europe provide the most readily applicable lessons for Eastern Europe. An alternative source is southern Europe, for in the postwar era societies from Turkey and Greece to Spain and Portugal have turned from authoritarian political regimes with substantial state control of the economy and a large subsistence agricultural sector to market economies with rising standards of living, albeit not yet matching northern Europe.

There is a wide choice of countries with functioning market systems, ranging from Sweden and Germany to the United States. European examples represent social market or social democratic systems in which public programs significantly restrict the freedom of action of firms in the market and assure a high level of social benefits for individuals irrespective of income. The United States represents, empirically as well as in the symbolism of neoclassical economists, a country wherein more freedom is given to firms to compete in the market and the level of publicly financed social benefits is not so high.

East Europeans tend to favor emulating such social democratic or social market countries as Germany and Sweden (table 5.2). The Soviet Union, which long dominated Eastern Europe, is totally rejected. The United States is the first choice of only a tenth of Hungarians, a seventh in Czechoslovakia, and less than one in three in Poland. Countries looked to for lessons are not traditional friends, for Germany has had a history of military aggression against its neighbors, and Sweden has been an aloof neutral state. Models for lesson-drawing are chosen on grounds of politically congenial values and demonstrated economic success.

It is impossible for one country to imitate another in every respect. The alternative is to draw on a repertoire of programs in effect in different countries. There is no shortage of advice. As a Moscow-based journalist writes:

> The ultimate models could be the United States, Sweden, West Germany or Japan. The transition models might be South Korea, Spain, or even Chile. The mix of tools might be French-style

TABLE 5.2
COUNTRY THAT EAST EUROPEANS MOST WANT TO BE LIKE

	CZECHO-SLOVAKS	HUNGARIANS	POLES	AVERAGE
Germany	31%	38%	37%	35%
Sweden	32	34	21	29
United States	14	10	30	18
Italy	9	9	0	6
France	5	2	7	5
Britain	3	3	3	3
Canada	3	0	0	1
Other	3	0	1	1
USSR	0	1	0	0.3

SOURCE: Freedom House, *Democracy, Economic Reform and Western Assistance; Data Tables* (New York: 1991), report of three-nation survey, table 154. "Don't know"s excluded.

planning, British-style privatization, Scottish/Irish-style encouragement of inward investment, Vatican-style capital-labor relations.

Mixed in the wrong combination they would make horrible cocktails. But they are all there on the shelf for trying after decades of no choice. (Lloyd, 1990)

BOUNDING SPECULATION THROUGH PROSPECTIVE EVALUATION

Lesson-drawing requires a prospective evaluation of *whether* a program that operates in one place today could work in another in the future. Whereas the past must be taken as a given, this is not the case with the future. If a prospective evaluation concludes that a program is likely to transfer successfully, then it may be adopted as is. If it identifies obstacles, the question is whether the obstacles are variables that can be altered or overcome, or do they constitute a veto on adoption.

Prospective evaluation involves speculation, but not unbounded speculation. It is not a test of a hypothesis, as in academic research, but the appraisal of a chain of reasoning (cf. Majone, 1991b: 298). It starts with a comparison between the actual conditions associated with a program already in effect and the presence or absence of these conditions in a second country. For example, if there is a proposal to build more hospitals to improve health conditions in a developing country, a prospective evaluation will emphasize the need for sufficient doctors, nurses, equipment, and drugs to be regularly available if it is to be effective. If these conditions are not met, the evaluation will stimulate a search for alternative health-care programs consistent with the country's resources.

The use of prospective evaluation can be illustrated by examining the British government's response to a decade of dissatisfaction with the low skill levels of young British workers. Through a process of trial and error, the British government in the 1980s decided to emulate the German dual system of vocational education and training, involving on-the-job training by employers and off-site training in technical colleges. The workings of the German system are open to empirical examination, for it has been in effect for generations. However, since vocational education and training institutions take a decade or more to register effects on the adult work force, only prospective evaluation can assess the new British program this side of the twenty-first century.

The critical step in undertaking a prospective evaluation is not learning how a foreign program works but applying knowledge gained abroad to one's own national circumstances. To read studies in German about its *Berufsbildungssystem* will provide a mass of details and improve one's linguistic abilities, but it will not tell policymakers what impact the program would have if transferred. To project that impact requires formulating the details of the German system as generic concepts that can be used as a model of the requirements of a dual system of education and vocational training, and applying it to British plans in order to determine if they actually meet conditions necessary for effectiveness (see Rose, 1991c).

A prospective evaluation of Germany today and the proposed British vocational education and training system must cover secondary schooling, training on and off the job, and employment after completion of training. Preparation at school shows one advantage of the German system. It provides a sound general education for the mass of youths, whereas Britain concentrates on a high educational standard for a minority. Prospective evaluation thus emphasizes the need to raise national standards of education for the mass of pupils or to incorporate an element of remedial or basic education in the vocational training program.

A second weak link identified by prospective evaluation is the absence in British workplaces of on-the-job trainers like the German *Meister*, a specially skilled master worker who supervises practical training and, as a skilled and well-paid adult, serves as a role model and mentor for young apprentices, whether they are training to be machine-tool operators, retail clerks, or bank tellers (Hamilton, 1990). Britain has never had a system of master workers, yet it is proposing to introduce a system of vocational training that requires hundreds of thousands of master workers. Prospective evaluation emphasizes that the new British program will not produce German-style results as long as it implies training without trainers. In the absence of the necessary number of qualified master trainers, the mass of young workers will receive a diluted and inferior training (Rose and Wignanek, 1990).

The purpose of prospective evaluation is to reduce failure through anticipatory feedback. Given advance notice of shortcomings that will be evident after the year 2000, British policymakers can act now to improve matters. They can develop programs to increase the supply of master workers in parallel with measures to increase the demand for training and match the expansion of training with the supply of skilled master workers. This would demonstrably produce more skilled workers by the year 2000 than the currently proposed program.

Lesson-drawing is not a mechanical set of deterministic procedures leading to unalterable conclusions. Obstacles to transferring programs are permanent only if present differences cannot be bridged in time. By thinking in terms of both time and space, a prospective evaluation not only identifies today's blockages but also highlights steps that can be taken now to draw an effective lesson about actions to improve the future.

6

Contingencies of Lesson-drawing

She would rather light a candle than curse the darkness.
— Adlai Stevenson of Eleanor Roosevelt

Although we cannot expect programs to be completely fungible, transferring easily from one government jurisdiction to another, equally, we cannot expect total blockage. The fact that a program is in effect somewhere else demonstrates that it is not inherently impossible to implement. To recognize the contingency of lesson-drawing is to accept the probabilistic nature of social science. In the face of uncertainty, Adlai Stevenson provides a cautious yet positive response: Rather than be discouraged by obstacles, it is better to look for conditions in which lessons can be drawn across time and space.

The critical task in lesson-drawing is to identify the contingencies that affect whether a program can be transferred from one place or time to another. The fungibility of programs is a matter of degree. As chapter 5 emphasized, it is usually easier to transfer programs within a nation than between nations. But many programs of national government have no counterpart at the state or local level. Insofar as common problems make possible common responses, national policymakers can learn something by looking abroad. In the case of interdependent defense and monetary programs, policymakers must pay attention to what other countries do, for the outcome of each nation's efforts depends also on what other nations do.

The uncertainties of lesson-drawing present opportunities as well as difficulties. This chapter addresses the challenge by setting out seven hypotheses about contingent influences on lesson-drawing across time and space. Each hypothesis concerns a particular element in the policy process that affects the fungibility of programs. Given the variety of public programs and contexts, it would be misleading to assign a precise quantitative weight to each influence, which can vary from time to time and place to place. The important concern of policymakers is not to assess general influences but to determine the significance of each element in a particular time and place.

The first three hypotheses identify qualifying conditions for lesson-drawing: A program should not be unique in most or all of its elements; it should not depend for its delivery on unusual or inimitable institutions; and its claims on the resources of law, public administrators, and money should be within the scope of the agency considering it. Within advanced industrial nations these conditions will normally be met.

The four hypotheses that follow are much more "iffy"; that is, the likelihood of their being met is highly variable, depending upon characteristics of the program and its specific context. The simpler the cause-and-effect structure of a program, the more fungible it is, for there is less to go awry in the process of transfer. The smaller the scale of change, the easier it is for a program to transfer, for administrative and political reasons. The greater the extent of interdependence of programs and asymmetries of power, then the greater the pressures for adapting programs in effect elsewhere. The greater the consistency of values between the program and the searcher, the more likely it is to transfer.

Uniqueness of Programs

Uniqueness emphasizes that a program is one of a kind, and thus incomparable. It implies that a program to promote mass transit in the United States has nothing in common with a program to do the same in Germany, or that a mass transit program in Boston has nothing in common with a mass transit program in another

American city. To prevent lesson-drawing, uniqueness must involve more than each program having a different history; a unique program must be literally inimitable.

A program consists of a number of interrelated elements defining its goals, regulations, finance, organization, entitlements, and so forth. In order to draw a lesson, a new program does not need to be an exact replica of every element of the original source. Functional equivalents may be substituted so that the new program does not lack anything essential in the original model.

Since a model identifies a number of elements in a program, it can be used to make a point-by-point comparison of the original program with a lesson drawn from it. This will show the extent to which the two have common elements.

Hypothesis 1. *The fewer the elements of uniqueness, the more fungible a program.*

A Ford Foundation competition to identify innovative programs in state and local government provides data to test the uniqueness of programs (Steinbach, 1990). Because innovations are by definition novel, the competition ought to give maximum attention to unique programs. Yet more than three-quarters of the forty prize-winning innovations are fungible (figure 6.1).

An example of a *unique* innovation is a program established in northern Alaska to maintain traditional values among a group of Eskimos. Alaska is not the only state with settlements of native Americans, but the culture and situation of Eskimos are very different from those of other Americans, native and non-native. Prima facie, a program that operates effectively among Eskimos in the Arctic Circle would not be expected to transfer to Indians in the deserts of Arizona and New Mexico or to urban dwellers. Only one of the forty Ford Foundation innovations was unique.

Most programs described as unique are not one of a kind; they are abnormal in the statistical sense, occurring in a limited number of places. Such programs are best described as *context dependent*. The typical context-dependent innovation is a program to

Contingencies of Lesson-drawing

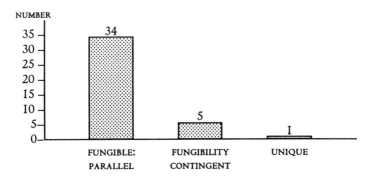

FIGURE 6.1

FUNGIBILITY OF INNOVATIVE PROGRAMS

SOURCE: Derived from a list of forty Ford Foundation awards for major program innovations, 1986–90. In Carol Steinbach, *Innovations in State and Local Government* (New York: Ford Foundation, 1990).

improve conditions for single-room occupants in residential hotels (it is only applicable in large cities) or to provide assistance to farm families (a measure suitable for rural areas). As long as the context is the same, then in principle a program can transfer. One-eighth of the innovations recognized by the Ford Foundation are context dependent.

Context-dependent programs reflect the coexistence of differences and similarities within nations. They are not capable of being generalized nationwide, yet within a given context, they can transfer readily. Moreover, if context is most important, then such programs can transfer across international boundaries. Programs for regional economic assistance are an example of context dependency across international boundaries. By definition, regional economic programs focus on areas that are economically behind other parts of a country. They must therefore exclude some regions within a nation. Since every country has regions that are below average economically, there is the potential for cross-national lesson-drawing.

Standardization, not uniqueness, characterizes most programs of government. A striking feature of innovations in state and local government is that five-sixths address problems for which there is a *parallel* in most jurisdictions of government. For example, the need to store land-use information is a common problem of local authorities, and many agencies of government are concerned with the control of water pollution. Parallels also exist for programs to reduce the prison population by allowing alternatives to incarceration. Even though each of the programs acclaimed by the Ford Foundation was unique when introduced in a particular place and time, each is in principle fungible because it addresses a problem with many parallels elsewhere. The logic of the awards is that innovations should spread rapidly because they represent desirable practices easily replicable elsewhere.

Standardization has been of major importance in the growth of government (Rose, 1988b). Common elements of a program are stipulated in laws, regulations, and professional training and practice. State laws, state legislative appropriations, state agency guidelines, decisions by state courts, and actions taken in Washington and by federal courts create common standards and obligations. Any mayor or governor who proclaimed that a program was unique might face awkward questions about whether the program conformed to state and federal laws. At the national level, some major programs parallel programs in other countries, for example, defense, diplomacy, and social security programs.

Comparing parallel programs offers policymakers a chance to move up the learning curve faster. Lesson-drawing is about analyzing variations in the responses of different governments to a parallel problem, in order to identify measures that can be undertaken with a high probability of bringing satisfaction because they have already done so elsewhere.

Institutions as Necessary Means

The influence of institutions on programs is confused by the different senses in which the word is used. Often the term is used to refer to formal and informal organizations and to patterns of behavior outside as well as inside government. For example, March and Olsen (1989: 17) define institutions to include "collections of standard operating procedures and structures that define and defend values, norms, interests, identities and beliefs." However, such broad definitions confuse the organizations delivering programs with informal behavior patterns and the programs themselves. Lumping everything together encourages the false belief that changing institutions necessarily changes program outputs.

Here the term institutions refers to formal organizations of government involved in implementing and delivering programs; colloquially, they are often referred to as public agencies, for they are means to the end of delivering programs. These executive agencies are not the only formal organizations in the policy process. Congress and interest groups promote or seek to block new programs and oversee implementation. However, the legislature and interest groups must normally exert influence through executive-branch agencies; they do not have hands-on control of service delivery.

Institutions are necessarily involved in the delivery of public programs. But even though institutions are necessary, it does not follow that they are important. Institutions are an intervening variable in the operation of programs; they constitute the "black box" between program outputs and the demands of the public and elected politicians for action (cf. Rose, 1984).

A new program can usually be administered in more than one way; insofar as this is the case, one institution can be substituted for another. The literature of public administration emphasizes that there is no one best way to organize a given public program. Many different organizational forms are consistent with a given goal (cf. Hood, 1986). Because of the indeterminate relationship between institutional forms and programs, governments have substantial leeway in drawing lessons from programs elsewhere.

The possibility of a program being fungible depends on the extent to which the delivery of a program requires a specific institutional form or, contrarily, whether there is substitutability between institutions. For example, health care may be delivered through a public, a not-for-profit, or a profit-making hospital or through a municipal, state, or federal hospital.

> Hypothesis 2. *The more substitutable the institutions of program delivery, the more fungible a program.*

Substitutability does not require an identity in form or procedures between institutions; it simply requires equivalence, that is, different institutions can perform the same functions notwithstanding some differences. The idea of equivalence is exemplified in the proliferation of IBM-compatible computers, which demonstrate their equivalence by running programs designed for IBM machines. Institutions do not need to be identical in order to be equivalent. As long as nothing is absent that is necessary and nothing is present that will prevent a program from working, then a lesson drawn from one place may be applied in another.

Within a nation, institutions tend to be similar and therefore not an obstacle for lesson-drawing by state and local governments. The federal Constitution lays down basic rules and obligations applicable throughout the nation; this ensures a degree of fundamental compatibility among state governments, and state constitutions ensure a substantial degree of compatibility among local authorities operating within a state. However, a constitution is a short document; most of its clauses do not concern organizations for program delivery, for they can be a century older than programs. Being subject to the same constitution is thus a necessary but not a sufficient condition for institutional compatibility.

Institutions represent clusters of political interests and values and may thus mobilize opposition to drawing a lesson inconsistent with their established interests. Strictly speaking, it is not the institution's form but its political clout that constitutes an obstacle to lesson-drawing.

Most new programs are implemented through established organizations. A new transportation measure can be assigned to the Department of Transportation, and a new military program to the Department of Defense. This reduces the cost in time, money, and inexperience of starting up a new organization. A new program is also likely to use established civil servants and standard operating procedures for those elements that are common to many activities of government.

The administration of public institutions is usually in the hands of expert officials, who tend to be at home with institutions specific to their program responsibilities, for example, prisons or libraries. Hence, when experts examine programs elsewhere, they are likely to find differences between overall systems of government less relevant than commonalities in service-delivery agencies. If there are significant differences, experts can use their knowledge to devise equivalent means to achieve a desired end.

Across nations, institutional differences are greater than within a nation, but common models create similarities between families of institutions. The reform of French institutions under Napoleon and the dominant position of France in early nineteenth-century Europe spread many French practices, particularly along the Mediterranean. The rise of Prussia was paralleled by many German concepts and institutions influencing the development of state structures in Central and Eastern Europe. The British Empire made Westminster and Whitehall institutions the pattern on four different continents.

National governments now station abroad officials concerned with programs once considered solely domestic. The U.S. Embassy in London has staff from forty-four different federal agencies attached to it. Only one-fifth of civilian government personnel stationed abroad are involved in what is defined as diplomacy (Duchacek, 1984: 23). Britain sponsors Commonwealth associations that draw together specialists from forty-nine different countries. Its Commonwealth Secretariat has divisions disseminating information about programs in fields as diverse as rural development, technology, health, law, education, and political institutions.

Institutions affect the fungibility of programs by their absence as much as by their presence. In default of an organization with the capacity to deliver a service, a new program cannot be adopted. A necessary first step in lesson-drawing is to see whether a government wanting to adopt a program has the institutional capacity to do so. This is particularly relevant in evaluating the transfer of programs from advanced industrial nations to developing countries and from market economies to Eastern Europe. For example, privatization programs presuppose the existence of a stock market and massive private-sector savings institutions. When these are absent, as has been the case in the nonmarket, centrally planned economies of Eastern Europe, such institutions must be created as a precondition of privatization or novel "giveaway" programs created to promote privatization.

Among advanced industrial nations, it is unusual for programs to be so dependent on a single institutional format that its absence makes it impossible to apply a lesson. Exceptionally, corporatist programs to manage wages and prices through tripartite institutions representing government, management, and labor presuppose the existence of business, trade, and government institutions with the authority to make binding agreements about wages and prices (cf. Lijphart and Crepaz, 1991; Schmitter and Lehmbruch, 1980). Such institutions can be found in some but not all OECD nations. In the absence of corporatist institutions, wage-price agreements are difficult to negotiate or to maintain. In the United States, for example, union membership is low, business enterprises are not integrated in peak nationwide organizations, and the executive branch and Congress are not organized to adopt a logically coherent set of wage-price guidelines. Hence, recurring efforts to introduce wage-price policies have been abandoned (cf. Goodwin, 1975).

The substitutability of institutions is evident in programs with similar goals operating through different means, as in education. Similarities in the goals of education—teaching literacy and numeracy and preparing youths for adult life and work—are of much greater importance than differences between federal systems that decentralize responsibility and unitary systems that give authority to central government; differences between countries in which the state church has or lacks a significant role in schools; or the complications of language and religion in a country such as Canada. Institutional differences in the delivery of education do not prevent the adoption of programs having common substantive goals.

Resources as a Constraint

Laws, public employees, and money are the three resources necessary to create public programs (Rose, 1985a). Public employees are needed to administer programs and deliver services. Money is required, for public officials must be paid; and some programs pay cash benefits directly to citizens, transferring money from the public treasury to those entitled to receive its benefits (Rose, 1985a). A program cannot be transferred if it cannot be stated in the form of a law. Many "lessons" drawn from observation of Japan are not fungible, for the conclusion is that Americans ought to behave like Japanese in ways that cannot be determined by legislation, for example, in labor-management relations in a factory.

Programs differ greatly in their mix of resources. Programs regulating marriage and divorce are law-intensive. By contrast, social security laws are money-intensive, for the immediate output is cash in the hands of the elderly. Health programs are both labor- and money-intensive, for they do not give money to the sick; instead, money is spent paying doctors, nurses, and hospital bills.

Fungibility requires not identical but equivalent resources. The United States Supreme Court usually recognizes that states can differ in details of programs as long as all are equivalent in upholding fundamental guarantees of the Constitution. A program in one country of the European Community does not have to be identical with what is done in all other nations to be in harmony with Community regulations.

Hypothesis 3. *The greater the equivalence of resources between governments, the more fungible a program is.*

To apply a lesson, a law must be drafted and enacted authorizing a new program. Within a country, equivalence in statutory language and procedures can normally be taken for granted. An act of Congress authorizing a program administered by states or cities creates nationwide compatibility by statute. States are allowed a measure of discretion in administration and sometimes in the amount of benefits provided. But the federal framework ensures that differences between states do not prevent the transfer of the program across state boundaries.

Between countries the language of acts is sure to differ, some legal terms are literally untranslatable, and there are differences in the extent to which laws specify details of programs (Blondel et al., 1969). Studies of comparative legal systems emphasize differences in legal philosophy between Roman law, which predominates in Europe and Latin America, and the English common-law tradition, found in many countries of the British Commonwealth and in the United States (Ehrmann, 1976: 13ff). This implies that it would be easier to transfer programs between Roman law countries, where programs are described in relatively abstract terms, than between common-law countries, where historical precedent is more important.

In fact, differences in drafting and interpreting laws rarely determine substantive program choices. It is possible to enact a health service or a social security system in either the common-law or the Roman law system. The technical difficulties of giving legal form to programs are secondary to political questions about the desirability of a program and political support for its enactment. The flexibility of legal systems is illustrated in Britain, where public programs must be suited to English courts and also to interpretation of the more Roman-based Scots' law. The substance of the program is the same (Rose, 1982: chapters 6, 7).

When legal services are the output of a program, considerable adaptation can be required to achieve equivalence. Although the potential threat to privacy of computerized data bases is a common problem for governments in Europe and the United States, data protection acts are not as fungible as computer programs. A study of the United States, Britain, West Germany, and Sweden, each with a somewhat different legal system, found: "The same policy problem has been met with the same set of statutory principles yet different methods of enforcement" (Bennett, 1988: 456ff). The American data protection act relies on individuals using the courts to protect their rights, in keeping with the individualistic and litigious nature of American law. By contrast, the European programs give public agencies greater responsibility for supervising and enforcing data protection, in keeping with greater trust in public servants as custodians of individual rights.

The European Community has adopted the concepts of harmonization to avoid differences in legal systems creating obstacles to the adoption of common goals and programs. The Community's operations are intended to secure harmony between national programs. The eighty-eight keys of a piano demonstrate that harmony can be achieved in many different ways. In the field of vocational qualifications, for example, the goal is transferability of qualifications across national boundaries for plumbers, electricians, and secretaries. However, this is *not* defined as uniformity in qualifications or methods of training. Instead, the Community promotes comparison of vocational qualifications, so that member states can become aware of what their competitors are doing and decide which elements of foreign programs they may wish to copy or adapt (CEDEFOP [European Centre for the Development of Vocational Training], 1989).

Most programs are labor intensive and money intensive rather than law intensive. Insofar as programs require employees with technical or professional expertise, there is no obstacle to lesson-drawing across space as long as an agency has an adequate number of trained professionals. Qualified highway engineers or public health officials can apply their expertise, whatever the original source of a program, and public agencies are major employers of technically trained personnel.

Bureaucratic efficiency appears to be a variable between states and cities, and between countries. New York City and Washington, D.C., are badly managed by comparison with good-government cities of the Pacific Northwest. States such as Minnesota and Wisconsin tend to have higher standards of competence than some southern states. Substantial differences in administrative effectiveness are also found between Scandinavian countries and Mediterranean societies. A necessary condition of Scandinavian satisfaction with big-spending welfare state programs is that officials administer the programs competently and not corruptly.

Insofar as public employees differ in efficiency, then in systems with inefficient or unresponsive bureaucrats it will be easier to transfer programs that move money to those with a clear legal entitlement, for example, pensions or child-benefit payments to mothers. Programs giving substantial discretion to service deliverers, such as social workers, will be less easy to transfer to places where bureaucratic effectiveness is low.

Money is a threshold resource. To adopt a program requires at least a minimum of money, and the bigger the claim on resources, the fewer the public agencies capable of funding big-spending programs. As chapter 5 showed, within the United States virtually every state has substantial cash resources—if it is prepared to make the tax effort. The same is true among most OECD nations. It is also possible to make a program affordable by adjusting the amount of money spent on benefits. For example, an unemployment benefit program can pay a large portion of lost wages for a long period of time or a small proportion for a short period of time, thus cutting costs greatly.

When policymakers say that money is lacking, this is usually because the will to tax and spend is absent, or the will to cut taxes is stronger than the will to spend. What this really means is that a program's purpose has a low political priority.

Most public programs claim only a very small percentage of the national product or the tax revenue of government. The great majority of federal programs cost between $50 million and $500 million dollars a year, 20 cents to $2 a year per American, or 0.004 percent to 0.04 percent of the federal budget. A program that requires a large amount of money, such as Social Security, does so because the payment to each individual must be multiplied by tens of millions of recipients. The existence of a few big-spending programs reduces the sum claimed by the median program.

Wealth is neither necessary nor sufficient for the transfer of many programs. Even if the cash cost of a program is low, it may be rejected if it is "costly" in political terms. And where money is short, as in some developing nations, the national government can finance military programs that cost large sums of money. Countries such as Chad, Ethiopia, and Somalia spend almost twice the percentage of their national product on arms that the United States does (cf. Sivard, 1987).

Insofar as money is an important resource for the transfer of programs, this should redirect rather than preclude lesson-drawing. Instead of looking to countries, cities, or states with resources far greater than their own, policymakers can turn their attention to places with similar resources in order to learn better ways of making policies.

Complexity of Programs

At its simplest, a program involves a direct link between a single cause and a single effect; if you want to achieve X, then do A. By contrast, a complex program involves a multiplicity of causes operating directly and indirectly to produce a multiplicity of effects. If you want to do X and Y, then do A, B, and C, which will achieve results indirectly through influencing F and G. But X and Y will also be influenced by H and I, which in turn reflect the influence of D and E, and have the unwanted consequence of producing Z. The more complex the program, the greater the likelihood that some determinants will be outside the control of individual decisionmakers or government collectively.

Complexity and its alternative, simplicity, vary substantially between programs. For example, if you want to decriminalize abortion, then repeal laws making it illegal. On the other hand, any program seeking to reduce teenage pregnancies will be more complex. Improving the labor market skills of youth is inherently complex. The goal can only be achieved as the joint outcome of different programs in such areas as education, employer choices, company investment, juvenile crime, and so forth. These programs interact with a multiplicity of influences in the home, the school, the peer group, the local labor market, and the national economy.

A relatively simple program can be made to appear extremely complicated if all the factors involved are anatomized in detail. Whenever complexity is emphasized, it becomes much more difficult to say whether a program can transfer. Policymakers seek simplicity, for the simpler a program is, the fewer actions that are required to introduce it and the fewer the assumptions that must be made in prospective evaluation. A program to regulate shopping by controlling the hours when shops can be open is inherently complex because it must take into account the preferences of shoppers and retailers, the working hours of men and women, the local economy, traffic conditions, and so forth. By contrast, a program to deregulate shop hours and let the market determine when shops open and close is simple, requiring only the repeal of laws and the leaving of decisions about actions and consequences to shop owners.

The inclination of policymakers to simplify, ignoring many consequences in order to concentrate on what is immediately important, makes it easier to transfer programs.

> Hypothesis 4. *The simpler the cause-and-effect structure of a program, the more fungible it is.*

The simplicity or complexity of a program depends on six attributes, which often are linked (see table 6.1).

A simple program will have a *single goal*, which may be ambitious or small, whereas a complex program normally has a multiplicity of goals. When there is a single object for a program, for example, reducing inflation, it is more likely to be fungible, for an anti-inflation program makes fewer assumptions about the national economic context than does a complex economic package seeking to reduce inflation, maintain full employment, and win the next election. Even though reducing inflation is often difficult, it is much less complex than simultaneously pursuing three different goals. A single objective avoids conflicts between competing goals, whereas a complex program requires tradeoffs between competing objectives, such as accepting a little more inflation for a little less unemployment, or vice versa.

The *fewer and more direct the causes* of a desired outcome, the greater is the likelihood that a program is fungible because there is less to transfer. For example, it is easier to reduce energy consumption by introducing a maximum federal speed limit of sixty miles an hour on public highways than to save energy by controlling the temperature at which families heat their homes. A speed limit can

TABLE 6.1

DIFFERENCES BETWEEN SIMPLE AND COMPLEX PROGRAMS

	SIMPLE	COMPLEX
Goal	Single	Multiple
Causes	One, direct	Many, often indirect
Empirical focus	Clear	Vague
Perception of side effects	Ignored	Internalized
Familiarity	Substantial	Novel
Predictability	High	Low

be directly monitored and enforced by the state highway patrol, whereas a limit on domestic heating would require elaborate enforcement procedures reaching into every house and apartment.

An *empirical focus* characterizes simple programs; their objectives can be reliably identified and verified. An empirical focus makes it possible to know what a program is meant to do, and to evaluate whether it has transferred effectively. For example, a program to ban smoking in public places can readily be monitored by observation, and the presence of tobacco fumes can be measured. By contrast, the goal of a program to improve relations between ethnic groups is diffuse and hard to measure empirically.

The *perception of side effects* increases the complexity of a program and makes it harder to transfer. A program can be simplified by concentrating on the removal of the immediate cause of dissatisfaction, making its evaluation self-contained. A program perceived as having many side effects in addition to its primary goal will be less fungible. If a highway program is viewed simply as a means of moving road traffic from one place to another, it is far easier to evaluate than if it is conceived as a means of altering the way in which people live and work and as having an impact on the natural environment.

Social science analyses are inclined to internalize both positive and negative side effects. By contrast, policymakers are inclined to externalize side effects, especially those that may be undesirable.

Other government agencies or the private sector are meant to carry the can, that is, take the responsibility. Ignoring side effects greatly simplifies the task of a policymaker.

> As decisionmaking is in fact practised, important consequences of policies under analysis are simply disregarded. Forthright neglect of important consequences is a noteworthy problem-solving tactic. What kind of important consequences are neglected? The answer is: any kind. (Lindblom, 1965: 145f).

Familiarity with a policy area simplifies analyzing cause-and-effect relationships and thus lesson-drawing. When much is already known about the way in which a program works in one state or nation, it is not so difficult to examine the same policy environment in a different place. By contrast, if a government is moving into a new area of policymaking, it will be unsure about what is happening in its own jurisdiction. Any judgment about how a program works in another place will involve even more uncertainties.

Predictability is never absolute in public programs because social phenomena involve more uncertainties than the materials of engineering sciences. A high degree of predictability may even be associated with low political significance. For example, a program to replace typewriters with word-processors in a public agency can be predicted to increase efficiency, but it is of no consequence politically. Economic programs, by contrast, are much more significant politically, but their consequences are less predictable. The greater the degree of unpredictability, the harder it is to draw a lesson about a program.

From a detached, analytic perspective, one can say that the most fungible programs are those that have a single goal, a single cause, and an empirically clear focus, ignore side effects, and are familiar and predictable. The above emphasizes that these attributes depend to a substantial extent on the way in which programs are perceived—and policymakers have considerable latitude in how they choose to perceive a measure. If a policymaker is satisfied with an existing program, alternatives are likely to be perceived as complex;

but dissatisfaction, once it arises, encourages simplification of lessons in order to make a single goal more attainable.

Scale of Change

Big changes are normally more difficult to achieve than small changes. By definition, a new program is a nonincremental form of change. However, novelty is not to be confused with scale; a new program can involve a small or a big difference in its claims on resources or in its impact. For example, drawing a lesson that leads to computerizing the payment of social security benefits is a much smaller policy change than a lesson that leads to changing the way in which social security is funded or benefits calculated.

> Hypothesis 5. *The smaller the scale of change resulting from the adoption of a program, the more fungible a program.*

Amending an existing program is likely to minimize the scale of change. An amendment can be added to an already established law and delivered by public employees of an agency accustomed to administering it. Amending a state sales tax by one cent may create a political dispute, but there is no technical obstacle to such an action; the fact that a sales tax is already in effect is proof that a program could have a tax at 3 percent instead of 2 percent. A proposal to introduce a sales tax in a state that does not have such a program is different; it is a change in kind, for the state must first establish procedures to collect the tax.

The scale of change is determined by the impact of a program on not only a society but also its government. A marginal change in an established social security program may affect far more people than the introduction of a specialized benefit, but it is administratively easy. However, introducing a new and specialized benefit will have a greater impact on public officials, for its implementation requires officials to do something for the first time.

The greater the number of already established programs, the bigger the scale of change, for a new program not only affects its target population directly but also has consequences for already established programs in the same policy area (Wildavsky, 1979: chapter 3). In an era of big government, there is a massive inheritance of programs from the past. Administrators and clients of established programs require more effort to convince of the advantages of adding a measure that may conflict with their own activities. This is true whatever the merits of the new program. As March and Olsen (1984: 737) emphasize, "History cannot be guaranteed to be efficient."

Cross-national lesson-drawing increases the scale of change because the program is not only new to the government adopting it but also operating in a new environment. Thus, introducing a nationwide federal value-added tax in the United States would be a much bigger change than amending or introducing a sales tax in a single American state. Sales taxes are familiar within American states, but even though the value-added tax has operated without difficulty in Europe and elsewhere, it would be a novelty for the federal government to administer.

Impact of Interdependence

Interdependence exists when a program in one jurisdiction is influenced by programs addressing a related problem in another jurisdiction; instead of being parallel, programs interact (cf. Keohane and Nye, 1989: 8). Even if policymakers ignore what is done elsewhere, in an interdependent system a program's outcome is the result of interactions between their actions and those of others.

> Hypothesis 6. *The greater the interdependence between programs undertaken in different jurisdictions, the more fungible the impact of a program.*

When what one government does about a problem influences others, there is an immediate incentive for policymakers to consider adopting a similar program or to learn how to compensate for the actions of other governments.

Interdependence is very evident in a metropolitan area, which contains a central city, a variety of suburbs, and several counties in one, two, or even three states. Decisions in one jurisdiction about programs for roads, housing, industrial development, and recreation facilities affect programs in other jurisdictions in the metropolitan area.

When there is interdependence between programs, one response is to standardize programs, as in roadbuilding; otherwise, roads would narrow and widen and superhighways start and stop every mile or two. Another alternative is to differentiate programs to achieve functional complementarity; one suburb may concentrate on industrial activities, another on offices and big apartment blocks, and a third on single-family residences. Competition is a third alternative: neighboring communities can differ in their combination of taxes and services, some offering good local services and higher taxes, while others offer lower standards of services and lower taxes.

Each state can study the programs of other states in order to adopt programs that give it a competitive advantage or at least impose no handicap. Traditionally, southern states have sought to attract industry from northern states by adopting pro-business programs that offer an incentive to firms to move away from states with pro-labor programs imposing higher taxes and more regulations. Insofar as a state wants to compete by trading up, it can adopt education and job-training programs that match the standards of the most liberal and progressive states.

In the interdependencies of the federal system, the national government has unique constitutional authority. The federal government can promote the adoption of a program at the state and local levels by using its resources of law, money, and information. It can impose a common program nationwide by federal statute. If it so preempts action, then the scope for lesson-drawing is reduced and uniformity becomes the norm. The federal government's field staff will focus on lessons about service delivery. If grants-in-aid are offered, meeting up to 90 percent of the cost, there is a financial incentive to adopt a program modeled along federal standards. If there is no compulsion and no money, then federal agencies are at a disadvantage in promoting lesson-drawing, for state and local officials usually do not turn to them for advice (Wright, 1988: 244ff).

The Supreme Court's power to interpret the Constitution reduces the scope for program differences. The Court has the power to mandate that states and city cease programs that create differences and adopt programs in effect elsewhere. In school desegregation, for example, the Supreme Court has endorsed programs such as busing and monitored their implementation. In the case of electoral redistricting, the Court has gone further, seeking a high degree of uniformity in procedures for creating electoral districts with equal numbers of voters.

When the success of a national program depends on actions outside its borders, functional interdependence blurs the distinction between foreign and domestic concerns. International affairs is no longer a specialist concern of diplomats; it also concerns policymakers seeking to remove domestic dissatisfaction. In addition to negotiation within their own government, policymakers must negotiate across national boundaries. "International conferences and organizations facilitate direct contacts among officials of what were once considered primarily domestic government agencies" (Keohane and Nye, 1974: 42).

In an era of empires, the imperial power was dominant in an interdependent system. In Africa, British colonies adopted institutions and programs based on Britain's, and French colonies had to use France as a source of lessons. After World War II the United States was able to use its position in Germany as an occupation power to influence the reform of German industry in keeping with American ideas about reducing the powers of industrial trusts (cf. Berghahn, 1986).

International interdependence is always evident in defense programs, for the effectiveness of a country's military force can only be judged in relation to its allies and its enemies. When interdependent nations differ greatly in the scale of their resources, smaller nations will be forced to attend to the activities of larger nations. As Canadian Prime Minister Pierre Trudeau explained to the National Press Club in Washington:

> Let me say that it should not be surprising if these policies in many instances either reflect or take into account the proximity of the United States. Living next to you is like sleeping with an elephant. No matter how friendly and even-tempered the beast, one is affected by every twitch and grunt. (Quoted in Hoberg, 1991: 108)

In economic policy, functional interdependence is transparent; international streams of commerce carry money, goods, and services across national boundaries. The dollar can be traded in Tokyo or London while Americans sleep; the profits of many American companies increasingly depend on sales abroad; and American consumers depend on imports for many household goods. Trade programs necessarily depend for success on the programs of other countries involved in the international exchange of imports and exports. National politicians may prefer to ignore international pressures but, as an OECD report (1990: 7) notes: "Even those countries which might have preferred to move more slowly have had to join the process of reform in order to avoid compromising their competitiveness."

The education and training of youths to become employable and skilled members of the labor force provides an example of how programs traditionally considered a problem of local schools and local employers have become internationalized as trade makes employers in different countries part of an interdependent and competitive system. A British government white paper on employment draws the moral: "Comparisons with where we were a few years ago are irrelevant, as are comparisons with what other British companies and organizations are doing. The comparison which counts is that with our overseas competitors, and that is to our disadvantage" (Cmnd. 9823: 1986: 2). President Clinton similarly stresses that the United States needs to look abroad for lessons in training workers (see, e.g., Hamilton, 1990).

The internationalization of markets creates interdependence between national economic policies. In an open international economy each nation's economy depends on what other countries do as well as on its own programs. As an OECD report (1988: 18) declares, "It is hardly possible in today's world to visualize any national situation in a purely closed-economy context." A country dissatisfied with its position must examine the programs of its competitors, as well as its own policies. Changes in economic programs are often forced on national governments that neglect "the importance of *paying due attention to developments and policies abroad....* What is sustainable can depend on what is happening abroad" (ibid.; italics in the original).

The European Community's creation of a Single European Market and its aspiration to create a common currency is an extreme example of national governments regarding interdependencies between economic policies as of great importance. They prefer to pool their authority to create new institutions to adopt common standards for programs that are fungible and pervasive in their impact across a dozen countries.

Values Shape Ends

Politicians are more concerned with values that define the ends of politics than with programmatic means. By contrast, civil servants and policy analysts tend to be concerned with using their expertise to design the means of public policy. Whereas a politician first thinks in terms of ideal goals, an expert looks at a program and asks: "Will it work?" (Rose, 1987a).

Politicians impose normative constraints on lesson-drawing. When they examine programs elsewhere, their perception is selective. They are inclined to see what they would like to see and to screen out what is uncongenial. Selective perception is matched by selective adaptation to circumstances. To describe screening as ideological is to miss the point. Some form of screening of possibilities is always necessary, and in a democracy it is appropriate that it is in accord with the political values of a popularly elected government.

Values only influence lesson-drawing if they are relevant to the policy issue at hand. Many values, for example, tastes in food or in dress, are remote from the everyday concerns of policymakers (Sabatier, 1988: 144ff). Political salience can also provide support for adopting a lesson, when it is seen as a means of realizing valued goals.

> Hypothesis 7. *The greater the congruity between the values of policymakers and a program's values, the greater its fungibility.*

A consensus simplifies the search for lessons, because there is widespread agreement about what can be considered and what should be ruled out. International studies of fundamental values concerning democracy, pride in nation, and overall life satisfaction consistently find a significant degree of consensus within and between countries. Differences are only in the size of the majority (Stoetzel, 1983). Any lesson consistent with consensual values will be supported by politicians of all parties. Attention can then concentrate on the instrumental element of lesson-drawing: Will a program that is effective elsewhere also be effective here? Differences of opinion are likely to be technical rather than normative and concern experts more than elected politicians.

Within a nation, there is substantial consensus about broad goals of government: Peace is better than war, full employment is better than unemployment, and stable prices are better than inflation. Disagreement can focus on priorities between competing goals or on the particular means of achieving consensual goals. In the United States, disagreements are often personal rather than programmatic, concerning which candidate is best able to attain general and noncontentious goals (cf. Downs, 1957; Stokes, 1963).

Consensus is a matter of degree. The statement "We want to achieve this goal" or "We don't want to pursue that objective" begs the question "Who is 'we'?" It may be an overwhelming majority of the electorate, a narrow majority, or a group that dominates because of its strategic position or mass apathy. To say that the majority of Mississippians do not want to copy the welfare programs of California or Wisconsin may be correct, but it does not mean that all Mississippians think the same.

If policymakers disagree about valued goals, then competitive lesson-drawing is likely to emerge. When dissatisfaction places an issue on the political agenda, the loose structure of policy networks encourages individual politicians to search in different places for different lessons. Committee hearings offer platforms to members of Congress with conflicting views, and a universe of two dozen advanced industrial nations offers ample scope for lessons. Advocates of change are most likely to use foreign examples to put a new program on the agenda, whereas opponents are more likely to draw negative lessons from abroad when proposals come to a vote (Robertson, 1991: 64).

Given disagreement about values, the critical question is not whether a program would transfer, but which program will get the votes needed for adoption? In such circumstances a policy analyst would do more to advance a program by campaigning for political support than by trying to refine the details of a proposal (Majone, 1991a). If a campaign to adopt a lesson fails, this will be a political defeat, but it does not prove that a proposal is not fungible.

Any political majority is inherently unstable, for it is a coalition of groups and interests. Instability is particularly striking in Washington, where coalitions must combine diverse and concurring majorities in the House, in the Senate, and in the executive branch. In the short run, instability may make it difficult to sustain a majority long enough to secure adoption of a new program. But in the long run values will only constitute a permanent veto on the transfer of a program if they are negative, consensual, and stable. The veto that the values of the current majority can impose on a particular lesson is real, but it is not permanent.

7

Time Turns Obstacles into Variables

It Can't Happen Here

— Ironic title of a novel by Sinclair Lewis

*M*any propositions that are true across space are not true across time. To say that a program that works in one place could not work in another confuses a truth about the present with uncertainty about the future. The fact that country Y does not have the program in effect today indicates that there *may* be difficulties in its immediate transference from country X. But this does not mean that a program cannot be introduced there in the future. The farther ahead one looks, the greater the degree of uncertainty, and thus, the greater the possibility of applying lessons from elsewhere.

At a given moment, it is easy to document obstacles to adopting a program based on experience elsewhere. A historicist argues against lesson-drawing on the assumption that present obstacles remain in place; the future is assumed to be determined by past events. In the short run, the political inertia of public agencies, employees, budgets, and laws makes programs "sticky" and difficult to alter. But every obstacle to change is sooner or later vulnerable to challenge.

In time, programs can become easier to transfer without any alteration in their intrinsic characteristics, as changes in policy environments remove obstacles. Paradoxically, the more influence attributed to the policy environment at a particular point in time, the harder it is to sustain the claim that today's obstacles will persist indefinitely into the future, for no policy environment is totally stable. Uncertainty about the future implies an openness to change. The length of time required to remove obstacles to lesson-drawing depends on the extent of difference between the "importing" and "exporting" governments.

Unexpected and undesirable changes in the policy environment widen the scope for lesson-drawing, as increased political dissatisfaction leads policymakers to reexamine their own past and speculate about the future. Dissatisfaction also leads to a search across space. When policymakers are dissatisfied with their current program, there is pressure to treat contingent conditions as obstacles to be overcome.

In the course of time, obstacles to lesson-drawing become variables. Models of the diffusion of a program from one American state to another assume that barriers to the introduction of a program sooner or later disappear. Across national boundaries, obstacles to lesson-drawing are likely to change more slowly, yet the same model of leaders and laggards applies. To argue that social programs in Europe today could not transfer to developing countries because they lack the money is true as far as it goes. But it also implies that as national income rises, social programs currently confined to a limited number of advanced industrial societies can be adopted more widely.

In the fullness of time, the *possibilities* for lesson-drawing expand; contingent obstacles become surmountable difficulties, or difficulties overcome. Even if a government wants to stand pat with its present repertoire of programs, the first section shows that changes in the policy environment force it to search for new measures or else experience a loss of effectiveness or a de facto change in goals. There always remains the prospect that in the course of time the influences identified in chapter 6 may become more favorable to applying lessons from elsewhere. Our conception of time and space is being transformed as time goes by. Changes within the United States have created discontinuities between the past and present and reduced differences between American states and regions. Even more dramatic changes have altered

America's place in the world. Whereas America once only looked inward, today it must look outward too. In the lifetime of most Americans great transformations have occurred in such monoliths as segregation in the Deep South and the Communist power structure in Eastern Europe; in time, many seemingly insurmountable obstacles can be overcome.

Responding to Changing Contingencies

In the present, nothing appears to have a tighter grip on policymakers than the dead hand of the past, the political inertia that maintains past programs and obstacles to transferring programs from elsewhere. Yet whatever the obstacles, in time they can be eroded by the future consequences of the more or less gradual compounding of current actions or by unexpected upheavals (cf. Rose and Davies, forthcoming).

CHANGE FORCES CHOICE IN A DYNAMIC POLICY ENVIRONMENT

Even if the programs of government remain the same, changes in the policy environment can force changes in a program, for its outcome reflects the interaction of what happens inside government and what happens in the external environment. In a free and open society policymakers cannot control all that happens in the policy environment. If the consequences of changes are benign, then a program will appear in a more positive light. Policymakers need do nothing but claim credit for outcomes that they have not caused.

However, changes in the environment can cause the effects of a program to deteriorate. What was good enough before becomes a cause of dissatisfaction. Policymakers must then respond to a stimulus to act imposed from outside government. The response can take the form of a search across time and space for a symbolic gesture to pacify the dissatisfied, a new program to attain better an existing goal, or a change in both the means and ends of a policy (figure 7.1).

If the environment changes for the worse, policymakers can ignore the change, reaffirming commitment to established programs and goals with the argument that difficulties are temporary and will soon go away. For example, if a monthly measure of inflation shows a rise, it can be dismissed as a blip caused by random fluctuations in the economy or statistical measures of performance. But if the cause is not part of a self-correcting cycle, inaction will result in routine programs deteriorating in effectiveness, and dissatisfaction will increase.

	IF ENVIRONMENT CHANGES, GOVERNMENT ...	
	KEEPS GOAL SAME	CHANGES GOAL
IF ENVIRONMENT CHANGES, PROGRAM ... REMAINS THE SAME	Deterioration	Symbolic gesture, passive acceptance
IF ENVIRONMENT CHANGES, PROGRAM ... CHANGES	Adaptation	Innovation

FIGURE 7.1
RESPONSES TO CHANGES IN THE
POLICY ENVIRONMENT

Since dissatisfaction is the result of a disequilibrium between aspirations and achievements, policymakers have the choice of maintaining an established program and altering its goal. The change of goals can be purely symbolic; this often happens in foreign policy, when there is little or no link between what one national government says and what happens in another country or continent. Alternatively, policymakers can passively accept change, lowering their aspirations to match whatever is happening. In the 1970s, historically high rates of inflation and unemployment were deemed "not unsatisfactory" because they were considered the best that could be obtained in the circumstances.

An alternative response to a deteriorating environment is to accept the change for the worse and adapt the means of policy to the new environment. The search for lessons can then proceed with clear terms of reference; the new program must be consistent with the established goal. Policymakers can disagree about which lesson offers the best means of responding to the changed environment, but there is no controversy about ends.

If dissatisfaction is intense and persistent, then the pressure is great to innovate, altering both the ends and means of programs. This is true whether changes in the policy environment occur gradually, as in the case of shifts in the demographic structure of the population, or abruptly, as in shifts in the price of oil.

A government searching for an innovative program cannot look to its own past. It must search across space or speculate about the future. The greater the dissatisfaction, the stronger the pressure to regard barriers to lesson-drawing as obstacles that must be removed, not as roadblocks preventing movement.

CHANGING CONTINGENCIES

By definition, a contingent obstacle to lesson-drawing is not a permanent obstacle. Whereas the preceding chapter emphasized influences on the present likelihood of lesson-drawing, the focus here is on changes making lesson-drawing easier in the future.

Because very few programs are unique, this condition is a very low barrier to lesson-drawing at present. It is likely to be lower still in the future inasmuch as social, economic, and technological changes reduce contextual differences within and between nations and the percentage of a country's population living in unique circumstances is reduced. *Parallel problems and programs* will be the norm both within the United States and among OECD nations.

Since *institutions* for program delivery tend to be substitutable, as long as this remains the case they are not obstacles to future lesson-drawing. Leaders of institutions, Heclo (1974) argues, are neither inherently conservative nor entrepreneurial; they view a particular lesson in terms of its impact on the institution's interests and values. They puzzle about anomalies and problems in the operation of their established programs. When political dissatisfaction increases, they are receptive to lessons that promise to remove problems that have been puzzling them as well as causing dissatisfaction among their clients.

In order to survive, institutions must be adaptable to changes in the policy environment. The institutions of British government are an extreme example of the capacity to adapt. It is the only way that government departments and Parliament could survive for many centuries. Throughout the twentieth century the institutions of the federal government have adapted to changes in policy, first in peacetime, then in wartime and its aftermath, and in an era of retrenchment today. They can be expected to be similarly adaptable in the twenty-first century.

Money is the most frequently cited *resource* that inhibits lesson-drawing; laws are insignificant obstacles, and standards of public employees and experts are usually adequate. Any ranking of states or nations by income, education, and other attributes necessarily shows that at a given moment in time, only one state or country can be first, and half must rank below the median in resources. Future projections based on rankings make it appear impossible for most political systems to "catch up," that is, to rank at the top.

But resource constraints on lesson-drawing are neither relative nor are they permanent. To introduce a particular program, a government needs a specific amount of revenue to finance it. Lack of revenue is an obstacle that sooner or later can be overcome by economic growth.

Even though the poorest states in the Union, Mississippi and Arkansas, are likely to remain below average in income for the next generation, as long as their economies grow at 3 percent a year, in a decade they will reach the average per capita income of the United States in 1992. If allowance is made for the lower cost of living in the South, then they can attain the level of resources needed to support all current programs even sooner. If the idea of a "rich" state is defined as the level attained by California or New York a decade ago, then many states below-average today have already reached that absolute standard of resources of richer states in 1980.

Compounding economic growth for almost half a century since 1945 results in many countries having the minimum income threshold required to finance programs once confined to a few. In 1950 the United States had an average per capita income more than two and one-half times the mean for advanced industrial societies. By 1990, twenty OECD nations had surpassed that standard of living and could afford "postwar American programs." Some Asian countries are reaching this level, too. When per capita income is high and rising in absolute terms, political values can still veto many lessons. But if values are not in conflict, then the question facing policymakers is not *whether* the country can afford a program in place elsewhere, but *when*.

In absolute terms, all OECD countries have far more resources than they had only two or three decades ago. Furthermore, more countries are in the process of achieving the material standards necessary to adopt programs that once were considered the preserve of the original members of OECD. In the Pacific Basin, countries such as Taiwan, South Korea, and Singapore have very high rates of economic growth and educated populations. In Eastern Europe former Soviet-controlled economies are anxious to catch up. Economic growth does not determine what a government does with its additional resources, but it does remove one obstacle to drawing lessons from the experience of advanced industrial nations today.

A secular increase in knowledge implies greater awareness of *complexity* and also a greater ability to decompose complex problems into their constituent parts. Systems scientists can construct far more elaborate models of programs and sensitivity test them for intended and unintended consequences through computer simulations. It is thus increasingly possible, if there is a demand from policymakers, to construct sophisticated models for the prospective evaluation of lessons.

The complexity of a program is not fixed; it reflects subjective perceptions and evaluations as well as objective phenomena. Insofar as some consequences are unpopular, the more widespread the knowledge of an extant program's effects, the easier it is to mobilize opposition to its adoption. An alternative response is to ignore complexity. Policymakers always have the option of taking a simple view of consequences. Policymakers may concentrate on a simple link between a few primary causes and a single effect. In the European Community, leaders in the drive for greater economic and political cooperation have not investigated in detail the complex interaction of hundreds of programs across the boundaries of twelve countries. Instead, they have emphasized a single pervasive vision that enables them to treat difficulties as secondary to the goal of a single European market.

At a given point in time, many obstacles to large-scale change must be taken as given. In education, even though a new university cannot be created overnight, it can be created within a decade. Many states responded to the 1960s explosion in numbers of college-age citizens by creating new universities. Programs to expand higher education enacted then have created hundreds of new institutions of higher education. In Europe many countries doubled the number of youths in higher education with the aid of lessons drawn from the United States.

The Federal Republic of Germany demonstrates both the prospects and difficulties of achieving large-scale change. At the end of World War II, all of Germany was devastated. West Germany drew on lessons from its own past to rebuild itself. Concurrently, the Communist regime of East Germany was forced to look to the Soviet Union for lessons. Four decades of division opened up a great gulf between the two Germanies. One had learned to create a democratic market system, and the other to exist as a nonmarket authoritarian regime. In a unified Germany, the government of the Federal Republic faces the task of undoing the inherited consequences of East Germany's adherence to Soviet practices and the challenge of drawing lessons from West German programs for use in the five new regions of an enlarged Germany.

Increased *interdependence* is a tendency of the growth of government. The more programs that government adopts, the greater the probability that some will interact with others within a broad policy area—primary, secondary, and higher education programs affect one another—and between policy areas (e.g., education, employment, health, and welfare programs affect one another). In addition, the probability increases that programs will become interdependent at different levels of government. As the federal government has grown, it has taken on responsibilities for programs delivered by state and local governments or by the private sector. In Europe, the European Community has programs in such policy areas as agriculture, regional policy, and industrial restructuring that are interdependent with national programs.

Increased economic interdependence increases the pressures for lesson-drawing. In the United States, the planned North American free trade area with Canada and Mexico is a commitment to interdependence through the market, a commitment that can force a review of private-sector as well as public policies in all three nations. The real though informal interdependence of the American and Japanese economies encourages Washington policymakers to look across the Pacific for lessons, as Japanese once looked to the United States.

The increased diffusion of information about living standards through the mass media is likely to increase the interdependence in popular expectations. Citizens who live in a poor part of a state or in a poor state may demand living standards similar to those of more prosperous fellow citizens. The result can be pressures for "territorial justice" (Rose, 1982: chapter 6), that is, common levels of benefit or policy achievements regardless of where a person lives. This creates pressure for adopting programs that are either uniform or based on lessons drawn from a common model.

Any obstacle to lesson-drawing arising from the *dominant values* of the government of the day is time-bound; it is valid only until the next election. If the election winner is substantially different in outlook from the administration that it replaces, dominant values can change overnight. Even if the party in office remains the same, the advent of a new leader is usually a time for welcoming new initiatives (cf. Bunce, 1981), and lessons drawn from programs elsewhere are immediately at hand.

If the values of the governing party fail to produce satisfaction, policymakers become more tolerant of lessons that they had initially ignored or opposed. The prospect of electoral defeat can lead the government of the day to make abrupt changes in the way in which it values lessons—if the alternative is to be accused of doing nothing in the face of mounting dissatisfaction.

The dominant values of the population can change in response to political events, and they can also change as one generation is replaced by another through the processes of birth, maturity, and death. Insofar as political values differ from one generation to the next, for example, on abortion or social policy, then programs that once seemed controversial are incorporated into a moving consensus, and lessons that were once deemed unacceptable can become accepted as commonplace.

As Time Goes By

When is as important as *whether* in the politics of lesson-drawing. To say that a lesson is not needed is a contingent statement; it means that everything appeared satisfactory the last time anyone looked at a specific program. It leaves open when or whether a gap will open between aspirations and achievement, stimulating policymakers to search for new measures. Lesson-drawing enables policymakers to escape from the tyranny of the present, which rejects anything that is not instantly applicable.

At a particular point in time it is often reasonable to conclude that a program that works elsewhere will not work here. But this judgment can also be stated thus: The time is not right for the successful transfer of a program. To stress the importance of timing implies that at some point in the future the time may be right to apply a lesson.

Policymaking is about waiting as well as about acting. Most moments are *not* the right time for putting forward a new program. There is a high opportunity cost for policymakers with many fires in their "In" tray to take on new commitments. Although ideas are always in circulation, what is lacking is the concatenation of events that creates the impetus for action. In the words of an interest-group official:

> When you lobby for something, what you have to do is put

together your coalition, and then you sit there and wait for the fortuitous event....

As I see it, people who are trying to advocate change are like surfers waiting for the big wave. You get out there, you have to be ready to go, you have to be ready to paddle. If you're not ready to paddle when the big wave comes along, you're not going to ride it in. (Quoted in Kingdon, 1984: 173)

Sooner or later the environment of every public policy is subjected to big waves. The bigger the wave, the more likely that a search of an organization's past will not suffice, and the greater the need to look elsewhere for lessons about what to do.

THE CHANGING WORLD OF AMERICA

Time is relative; the motto of a British prime minister, Harold Wilson, was: "A week is a long time in politics." A White House aide saw events moving faster still: "This is the kind of place where everything hits the fan before 9 o'clock in the morning." For elected politics, the electoral cycle imposes an outer limit on calculations. Each member of the House of Representatives faces reelection every two years. A president has a four-year term of office, but exploiting the first hundred days and surviving a barrage of unfavorable opinion polls foreshortens the time horizon of the White House.

Whereas politicians may measure time in days or weeks, history records the cumulative effect of decades of collective effort by policymakers, alive and dead. It also records the cumulative effect of changes in American society.

On the eve of the twenty-first century, the United States cannot look solely to the past for ideas about public policy, for the differences between past and present are too great to give confidence that what worked forty or seventy-five years ago will work in the next century. There is no need to have a single watershed date before which lessons cannot be drawn. The purpose determines the relevance of a date: the start of the New Deal in 1933; America's entry into World War II; the 1954 Supreme Court decision ending desegregation; the rise and fall of the War on Poverty in the 1960s; the election of Ronald Reagan in 1980 or the inauguration of President Clinton in 1993. Beyond a certain point, discontinuities make it impossible to treat the status quo ante as much the same as the present and future.

Even though space is fixed in a geographical sense, as time goes by our subjective idea of what is near at hand changes. In the days of the horse and buggy, cities and counties tended to be self-contained units. Then distances started shrinking. The locomotive and the motor car made intrastate and interstate communication feasible. Officials throughout a state could easily meet. Washington was no longer completely remote. The rise of national media—the press and magazines, then radio and television—made it easy to spread ideas nationally. Not so long ago it took up to twenty-four hours for a member of Congress from the Midwest to return from Washington to his or her district and three days to travel from the West Coast to the capital. Now, Washington airports have a continuous flow of people circulating from around the country, and most members of Congress can be in their offices at lunch and in their districts for evening meetings.

The world of which the United States is a part is changing too. Since the time of Alexis de Tocqueville, foreign visitors have come to the United States seeking positive or negative lessons. Today, foreigners continue to come to America to learn—but more often as students of science and technology than of American political institutions. Today, Japan is an exemplar to developing nations seeking to modernize their economies. Germany is looked to for lessons about combining economic growth with a stable currency. Many European countries have lower crime rates and fewer urban problems than the United States. Collectively, two dozen advanced industrial nations offer more lessons for policymakers to choose from than does any one nation, including the United States.

The travels of the president demonstrate how the world is shrinking. Until the beginning of the twentieth century no president had ever been abroad while in office. It was only in the Eisenhower administration that it became normal for a president to go abroad to meet firsthand with foreign leaders. Presidents since the time of John F. Kennedy have treated the White House as a global office and often have shown limited interest in domestic politics (Rose, 1991e).

The idea that "all politics is local" is now a half-truth. Although foreigners do not have votes in American elections, what happens elsewhere can impact domestic programs. Members of Congress from farm districts find that what is decided in Brussels about the European Community's agricultural imports affects their constituents. Politicians representing car manufacturing districts know that the economic well-being of their constituents is affected by what happens in Japan and by the lessons that Detroit car makers learn from Japanese competition. When Americans buy more goods from foreigners than foreigners buy from the United States, it is unconvincing to argue that America has nothing to learn from the rest of the world.

NEVER SAY NEVER IN POLITICS

Politicians learn from experience that dogmatically dismissing an idea is dangerous, for the time may come when a program once labeled undesirable or unworkable suddenly promises to dispel dissatisfaction.

Great political changes can be accomplished within a relatively short time. During the New Deal of Franklin D. Roosevelt, the Deep South was a standing example of the past controlling the present. A history of slavery, rebellion, and defeat and a political system that denied rights to blacks appeared a total block to many programs. As late as the 1960s George Wallace could be elected governor of Alabama with the slogan: "Segregation now and forever."

Yet race relations in the South have been transformed in a generation. The first move to dislodge the seemingly implacable wall of segregation was the nonviolent bus boycott in Montgomery, Alabama, led by Martin Luther King, Jr. There was nothing in the history of the American South that could offer King a lesson about how to overcome segregation, and much to indicate that the task was hopeless. King searched for lessons across time and space; he studied the nonviolence practiced by Mahatma Gandhi in resisting the British Raj in India and the use of nonviolence in a bus boycott in Johannesburg, South Africa.

Nonviolent protest has since spread across continents. In East Germany in 1989, hundreds of thousands of demonstrators peacefully massed in Leipzig, in Dresden, and in East Berlin to show their rejection of a heavily armed totalitarian system. Even though the East German Communist regime appeared a fortress resistant to change, it too fell.

In the 1990s Eastern Europe demonstrates that even obstacles as apparently unyielding as a Communist regime can collapse abruptly. The distance between Eastern and Western Europe is not a matter of space, for some cities of Eastern Europe, such as Prague, are actually to the west of some cities nominally assigned to the West, such as Vienna and Stockholm, and the geographical ties of a country such as Germany are as much with Eastern Europe as with the West.

The distances between Eastern and Western Europe are today a function of time. The old regimes have left behind massive dissatisfaction with economic and political institutions and created a demand for lessons from abroad. East European governments are desperately searching for programs that may enable them to catch up with democratic market societies. The legacy of the past has imposed handicaps that cannot be resolved in the short span of time between two elections. Yet a start must be made.

No one has a right to tell people seeking democracy and a market economy that they can never achieve this goal and that nothing can be learned from experience elsewhere, whether of democratic market systems or postcommunist societies. As Lawrence Summers, chief economist of the World Bank told a meeting of Baltic leaders (1991: 6): "Many of the world's greatest economic success stories were written off much too soon. In many economic situations, including this one, things take longer to happen than you think they will; then they happen faster than you expect them to."

Our contacts with other cities, states, and nations are increasing. When dissatisfaction arises at home, there is no reason to ignore the way in which governments elsewhere respond to common problems. There is enough trade in the marketplace of ideas to show that some public programs can transfer effectively. The critical issues of lesson-drawing are not whether we can learn anything elsewhere, but when, where, and how we learn.

References

ACIR (Advisory Commission on Intergovernmental Relations). 1987. *Significant Features of Fiscal Federalism.* Washington, D.C.
———. 1991. *Significant Features of Fiscal Federalism, Volume 2: Revenues and Expenditures.* Washington, D.C.
Aho, Michael, and Marc Levinson. 1988. *After Reagan: Confronting the Changed World Economy.* New York: Council on Foreign Relations.
Amsden, Alice H. 1990. *Asia's Next Giant: South Korea and Late Industrialization.* Oxford: Oxford University Press.
Anderson, Charles W. 1978. "The Logic of Public Problems: Evaluation in Comparative Policy Research." In *Comparing Public Policies,* edited by Douglas Ashford, 19–42. Beverly Hills, Calif.: Sage.
Arnold, R. Douglas. 1979. *Congress and the Bureaucracy: A Theory of Influence.* New Haven: Yale University Press.
Arthur, W.B. 1988. "Self-Reinforcing Mechanisms in Economics." In *The Economy as an Evolving Complex System,* edited by P.W. Anderson, K.J. Arrow, and D. Pines, 5: 9–32. Santa Fe, N.M.: Santa Fe Institute Studies in the Sciences of Complexity/Addison-Wesley.
Bennett, Colin J. 1988. "Different Processes, One Result: The Convergence of Data Protection Policy in Europe and the United States." *Governance* 1(4): 162–83.
———. 1988a. "Regulating the Computer: Comparing Policy Instruments in Europe and the United States." *European Journal of Political Research* 16: 437–66.
———. 1990. "The Formation of a Canadian Privacy Policy: The Art and Craft of Lesson-Drawing." *Canadian Public Administration* 33(4): 551–70.
———. 1991. "How States Utilize Foreign Evidence." *Journal of Public Policy* 11(1): 31–54.
———. 1991a. "What Is Policy Convergence and What Causes It?" *British Journal of Political Science* 21(2): 215–34.

Berghahn, Volker R. 1986. *The Americanization of West German Industry, 1945–1973.* New York: Berg.
Berry, Frances Stokes, and William D. Berry. 1990. "State Lottery Adoptions as Policy Innovations." *American Political Science Review* 84(2): 395–416.
Blondel, Jean, et al. 1969. "Legislative Behaviour: Some Steps towards a Cross-National Measurement." *Government and Opposition* 5(1): 67–85.
Bobrow, D., and J. Dryzek. 1987. *Policy Analysis by Design.* Pittsburgh: University of Pittsburgh Press.
Braybrooke, David, and C.E. Lindblom. 1963. *A Strategy of Decision.* New York: Free Press.
Brudney, Jeffrey L., and F. Ted Hebert. 1987. "State Agencies and their Environments." *Journal of Politics* 49(2): 186–206.
Brudney, Jeffrey L., F. Ted Hebert, and Deil S. Wright. 1990. "Charting the Administrative Dimension of State Government." Paper presented at the annual meeting of the Southwestern Political Science Association, Fort Worth, 28–31 March.
Bruno, Michael, and J. Sachs. 1985. *Economics of Worldwide Stagflation.* Oxford: Oxford University Press.
Bruszt, Laszlo, and Janos Simon. 1991. *Codebook of the International Survey of Political Culture during the Transition to Democracy.* Budapest: Erasmus Foundation for Democracy.
Bunce, Valerie. 1981. *Do New Leaders Make a Difference?* Princeton: Princeton University Press.
Camdessus, Michel. 1989. "Role of Government Is to Create Favorable Environment for Growth." *IMF Survey,* 11 December, 369–74.
Carlson, B.L., Johanna Koenig, and G.L. Reid. 1986. *Lessons from Europe: The Role of the Employment Security System.* Washington D.C.: National Governors' Association.
CEDEFOP (European Centre for the Development of Vocational Training). 1989. "Europe: A Labour Market without Frontiers." *Vocational Training* no. 3, 1–44.
Clark, Jill. 1985. "Policy Diffusion and Program Scope." *Publius* 15(4): 61–70.
Clemens, Elisabeth S. 1990. "Secondhand Laws: Patterns of Political Learning among State Governments and Interest Groups." Paper presented at the annual meeting of the American Political Science Association, San Francisco.
Cmnd. 9823. 1986. *Working Together—Education and Training.* London: Her Majesty's Stationery Office.
Cohen, Michael D., James G. March, and Johan P. Olsen. 1972. "A Gar-

bage-Can Model of Organizational Choice." *Administrative Science Quarterly* 17(1): 1–25.

Cohen, Michael D., and Robert Axelrod. 1984. "Coping with Complexity: The Adaptive Value of Changing Utility." *American Economic Review* 74(1): 30–41.

Collier, David, and Richard E. Messick. 1975. "Prerequisites versus Diffusion: Testing Alternative Explanations of Social Security Adoption." *American Political Science Review* 69(4): 1299–1315.

Cooper, Richard N. 1989. "International Cooperation in Public Health as a Prologue to Macroeconomic Cooperation." In *Can Nations Agree?* edited by R.N. Cooper et al., 178–254. Washington, D.C.: Brookings Institution.

Council of State Governments. 1990. *The Book of the States: 1990–91*. Lexington, Ky.

Cyert, R., and J.G. March. 1963. *A Behavioral Theory of the Firm*. Englewood Cliffs, N.J.: Prentice-Hall.

Day, Patricia, and Rudolf Klein. 1989. "Interpreting the Unexpected: The Case of AIDS Policymaking in Britain." *Journal of Public Policy* 9(3): 337–54.

Dempster, M.A.H., and Aaron Wildavsky. 1979. "On Change: or, There Is No Magic Size for an Increment." *Political Studies* 27: 371–89.

Dery, David. 1982. "Evaluation and Problem Redefinition." *Journal of Public Policy* 2(1): 23–30.

Destler, I.M. 1986. *American Trade Politics: System under Stress*. Washington D.C.: Institute for International Economics.

Deutsch, K.W. 1963. *The Nerves of Government*. New York: Free Press.

Dogan, Mattei, and Dominique Pelassy. 1984. *How to Compare Nations: Strategies in Comparative Politics*. Chatham, N.J.: Chatham House.

Dogan, Mattei, and Dominique Pelassy. 1990. *How to Compare Nations: Strategies in Comparative Politics*. 2d ed. Chatham, N.J.: Chatham House.

Doig, Jameson, and Erwin C. Hargrove, eds. 1987. *Leadership and Innovation: A Biographical Perspective on Entrepreneurs in Government*. Baltimore: Johns Hopkins University Press.

Dommergues, P., H. Sibille, and E. Wurzburg. 1989. *Mechanisms for Job Creation: Lessons from the United States*. Paris: Organisation for Economic Cooperation and Development.

Douglas, Mary. 1987. *How Institutions Think*. London: Routledge and Kegan Paul.

Downs, Anthony. 1957. *An Economic Theory of Democracy*. New York: Harper and Row.

Duchacek, Ivo. 1984. "Federal States and International Relations." *Publius* 14(4): 5–32.
Eckstein, Harry. 1992. *Regarding Politics: Essays on Political Theory, Stability, and Change.* Berkeley: University of California Press.
Economica. 1986. "Unemployment." A special supplement edited by Charlie Bean, Richard Layard, and Stephen Nickell, 53, no. 210 (S).
Edelman, Murray. 1964. *The Symbolic Uses of Politics.* Urbana: University of Illinois Press.
Ehrmann, Henry W. 1976. *Comparative Legal Cultures.* Englewood Cliffs, N.J.: Prentice-Hall.
Enthoven, Alain C. 1990. "What Can Europeans Learn from Americans?" In *Health Care Systems in Transition,* edited by Organization for Economic Cooperation and Development, 57–74. Paris: OECD Social Policy Studies no. 7.
Etheredge, Lloyd S. 1981. "Government Learning: An Overview." In *The Handbook of Political Behavior,* edited by Samuel L. Long, vol. 2, 73–161. New York: Plenum Press.
———. 1985. *Can Governments Learn?* New York: Pergamon Press.
Etzioni, Amitai. 1985. "Making Policy for Complex Systems: A Medical Model for Economics." *Journal of Policy Analysis and Management* 4(3): 383–95.
———. 1988. *The Moral Dimension: Toward a New Economics.* New York: Free Press.
———. 1991. "Eastern Europe: The Wealth of Lessons." *Challenge* 34 (4): 3–10.
Eurobarometer. 1989. *Eurobarometer: Trend Variables, 1974–1989.* No. 32 Appendix. Brussels: European Commission.
Eyestone, Robert. 1977. "Confusion, Diffusion and Innovation." *American Political Science Review* 71(2): 441–47.
Fenno, Richard F., Jr. 1978. *Home Style: House Members in their Districts.* Boston: Little, Brown.
Fesler, James W. 1959. "Editorial Comment: Across Time and Space." *Public Administration Review* 19 (Summer): 215.
Flora, Peter, and A.J. Heidenheimer, eds. 1981. *The Development of Welfare States in Europe and America.* New Brunswick, N.J.: Transaction Books.
Freeman, Gary P. 1985. "National Styles and Policy Sectors: Explaining Structured Variation." *Journal of Public Policy* 5(4): 467–96.
Frey, B.S., W.W. Pommerehne, F. Schneider, and G. Gilbert. 1984. "Consensus and Dissension Among Economists: An Empirical Enquiry." *American Economic Review* 74: 986–94.

References

Glaser, William A. 1987. *Paying the Hospital.* San Francisco: Jossey-Bass.

——. 1988. *Financial Decisions in European Health Insurance: Lessons for the United States.* New York: New School for Social Research, Graduate School of Management.

Goode, Richard. 1984. *Government Finance in Developing Countries.* Washington, D.C.: Brookings Institution.

Goodman, John B. 1991. "The Politics of Central Bank Independence." *Comparative Politics* 23(2): 329–50.

Goodwin, Craufurd D., ed. 1975. *Exhortation and Controls: The Search for a Wage-Price Policy 1945–71.* Washington, D.C.: Brookings Institution.

Grady, Dennis O., and Keon S. Chi. 1990. "The Role of External Actors in the Formulation and Implementation of State Government Initiatives." Paper presented at the annual meeting of the American Political Science Association, San Francisco.

Gray, Virginia L. 1973. "Innovation in the States: A Diffusion Study." *American Political Science Review* 67(4): 1174–93.

Grupp, Fred W., Jr., and Alan R. Richards. 1975. "Variations in Elite Perceptions of American States as Referents for Public Policymaking." *American Political Science Review* 69(3): 850–58.

Haas, Ernst B. 1990. *When Knowledge Is Power: Three Models of Change in International Organizations.* Berkeley: University of California Press.

Haas, Peter M. 1990. *Saving the Mediterranean: The Politics of International Environmental Cooperation.* New York: Columbia University Press.

Haig, Alexander M. 1990. "Gulf Analogy: Munich or Vietnam?" *New York Times,* December 10.

Hall, Peter A., ed. 1989. *The Political Power of Economic Ideas.* Princeton: Princeton University Press.

Hamilton, Stephen F. 1990. *Apprenticeship for Adulthood.* New York: Free Press.

Hartley, L.P. 1953. *The Go-between.* London: Hamish Hamilton.

Heald, Anne. 1988. "Merchandising Ideas: Continent to Community." *The Entrepreneurial Economy Review* 7(1): 13–16.

Heclo, Hugh. 1974. *Modern Social Politics in Britain and Sweden.* New Haven: Yale University Press.

——. 1977. *A Government of Strangers.* Washington, D.C.: Brookings Institution.

——. 1978. "Issue Networks and the Executive Establishment." In *The New American Political System,* edited by A.S. King, 87–124. Washington D.C.: American Enterprise Institute.

Hedberg, Bo. 1981. "How Organizations Learn and Unlearn." In *Handbook of Organizational Design,* edited by Paul C. Nystrom and William H. Starbuck, 3–27. New York: Oxford University Press.

Heidenheimer, Arnold J., Hugh Heclo, and Carolyn T. Adams. 1990. *Comparative Public Policy.* 3d ed. New York: St. Martin's Press.

Hirschman, A.O. 1958. *The Strategy of Economic Development.* New Haven: Yale University Press.

Hoberg, George. 1986. "Technology, Political Structure and Social Regulation." *Comparative Politics* 18(3): 357–76.

———. 1991. "Sleeping with an Elephant: the American Influence on Canadian Environmental Legislation." *Journal of Public Policy* 11(1): 107–32.

Hood, Christopher. 1983. *The Tools of Government.* London: Macmillan.

———. 1986. *Administrative Analysis.* Brighton: Wheatsheaf.

Hood, Christopher, and Michael Jackson. 1991. *Administrative Argument.* Aldershot: Dartmouth.

Howard, Michael. 1991. *The Lessons of History.* Oxford: Oxford University Press.

IIASA (International Institute for Systems Analysis). 1990. "The Soviet Economic Crisis: Steps to Avert Collapse." In *Options* (December), 5–8. Laxenberg, Austria.

Inglehart, Ronald. 1977. *The Silent Revolution.* Princeton, N.J.: Princeton University Press.

International Monetary Fund. 1991. *World Economy Outlook: May 1991.* Washington D.C.

Johnstone, Dorothy. 1975. *A Tax Shall Be Charged.* London: Civil Service Studies, Her Majesty's Stationery Office.

Jordan, Fred. 1990. *Innovating America.* New York: Ford Foundation.

Kearl, J., C. Pope, G. Whiting, and L. Wimmer. 1979. "A Confusion of Economics?" *American Economic Review: Papers and Proceedings* 69(2): 28–37.

Kelman, Steven. 1981. *What Price Incentives? Economists and the Environment.* Boston: Auburn House.

Keohane, Robert O., and Joseph S. Nye. 1974. "Transgovernmental Relations and International Organizations." *World Politics* 27(1): 39–62.

———. 1989. *Power and Interdependence.* 2d ed. Glenview, Ill.: Scott Foresman/Little Brown.

Kerr, Clark. 1983. *The Future of Industrial Societies.* Cambridge, Mass.: Harvard University Press.

Khanna, Vikram R. 1991. "Economists Discuss Eastern Europe, Uruguay Round and European Monetary Union." *IMF Survey*, 30 September, 277–80.

Kincaid, John. 1984. "American Governors in International Affairs." *Publius* 14(4): 95–114.

King, Anthony. 1973. "Ideas, Institutions and Policies of Governments:

A Comparative Analysis." *British Journal of Political Science* (two parts) 3(3): 291–314, and 3(4): 409–24.
Kingdon, John W. 1984. *Agendas, Alternatives, and Public Policies.* Boston: Little, Brown.
Klingman, David. 1980. "Temporal and Spatial Diffusion in the Comparative Analysis of Social Change." *American Political Science Review* 74(1): 123–37.
Kochen, Manfred, and Karl W. Deutsch. 1980. *Decentralization.* Cambridge, Mass.: Oelgeschlager, Gunn and Hain.
Kohn, Melvin L., ed. 1989. *Cross-National Research in Sociology.* Newbury Park, Calif.: Sage.
Koop, C. Everett. 1990. "U.S. Health System Needs Profound Change." *Modern Health Care,* 4 June.
Kuhn, Thomas G. 1962. *The Structure of Scientific Revolutions.* Chicago: University of Chicago Press.
Libowitz, Steve. 1991. "The Currency Doctor." *Johns Hopkins Magazine* 43 (5): 47–49.
Lichfield, John. 1991. "U.S. Insomniacs Phone the Gorbachev-Yeltsin TV Show." *The Independent* (London), 7 September.
Lijphart, Arend, and Markus M.L. Crepaz. 1991. "Corporatism and Consensus Democracy in Eighteen Countries." *British Journal of Political Science* 21(2): 235–47.
Lindblom, C.E. 1965. *The Intelligence of Democracy.* New York: Free Press.
Linder, S.H., and B. Guy Peters. 1989. "Instruments of Government: Perceptions and Contexts." *Journal of Public Policy* 9(1): 35–58.
Linz, Juan J. 1990. "The Perils of Presidentialism." *Journal of Democracy* 1(1): 51–70.
Lipset, S.M. 1990. *A Continent Divided.* New York: Routledge.
Lloyd, John. 1990. "The Kick in the Capitalist Cocktail." *Financial Times,* 15 August.
Lutz, James M. 1989. "Emulation and Policy Adoptions in the Canadian Provinces." *Canadian Journal of Political Science* 22(1): 147–54.
Mackie, T.T., and Richard Rose. 1991. *The International Almanac of Electoral History.* 3d ed. Washington D.C.: Congressional Quarterly.
McCloskey, Donald N. 1984. "The Literary Character of Economics." *Daedalus,* Summer, 97–119.
Majone, Giandomenico. 1989. *Evidence, Argument and Persuasion in the Policy Process.* New Haven: Yale University Press.
———. 1991. "Cross-National Sources of Regulatory Policymaking in Europe and the United States." *Journal of Public Policy* 11(1): 79–106.
———. 1991a. "Research Programs and Action Programs." In *Social*

Sciences and Modern States, edited by P. Wagner, C.H. Weiss, B. Wittrock, and H. Wollmann, 290–306. New York: Cambridge University Press.

March, James G., and Johan P. Olsen. 1984. "The New Institutionalism: Organizational Factors in Political Life." *American Political Science Review* 78(3): 734–49.

———. 1989. *Rediscovering Institutions*. New York: Free Press.

Marmor, Theodore C. 1983. *Political Analysis and American Medical Care*. New York: Cambridge University Press.

Marmor, Theodore C., with Philip Fellman. 1986. "Policy Entrepreneurship in Government." *Journal of Public Policy* 6(3): 225–54.

May, Ernest R. 1973. *"Lessons" of the Past: The Use and Misuse of History in American Foreign Policy*. New York: Oxford University Press.

Merton, Robert K. 1957. *Social Theory and Social Structure*. Revised and enlarged edition. Glencoe, Ill.: Free Press.

Miller, Cheryl M. 1988. "State Administrator Perceptions of the Policy Influence of Other Actors: Is Less Better?" *Public Administration Review* 47(3): 239–45.

Muniak, Dennis. 1985. "Policies that 'Don't Fit': Words of Caution on Adopting Overseas Solutions to American Problems." *Political Studies Journal* 14(1): 1–19.

Nadler, Leonard. 1984. "What Japan Learned from the U.S.—That We Forgot to Remember." *California Management Review* 26(4): 46–61.

Nailor, Peter. 1991. *Learning from Precedent in Whitehall*. London: Institute of Contemporary British History and Royal Institute of Public Administration.

Neustadt, Richard E. 1960. *Presidential Power*. New York: John Wiley.

Neustadt, Richard E., and Harvey Fineberg. 1983. *The Epidemic that Never Was*. New York: Vintage.

Neustadt, Richard E., and Ernest R. May. 1986. *Thinking in Time: The Uses of History for Decision Makers*. New York: Free Press.

Nowak, Stefan. 1989. "Comparative Studies and Social Theory." In *Cross-National Research in Sociology*, edited by Melvin L. Kohn, 34–56. Newbury Park, Calif.: Sage.

Organisation for Economic Cooperation and Development. 1985. *Social Expenditure, 1960–1990*. Paris.

———. 1988. *Why Economic Policies Change Course: Eleven Case Studies*. Paris.

———. 1990. *Progress in Structural Reform*. Paris. Supplement to *Organisation for Economic Cooperation and Development Economic Outlook* 47.

———. 1991. *Historical Statistics, 1960–1989*. Paris.

References

Pellegrin, Jean-Pierre. 1989. "Local Initiatives for Enterprise." *Organisation for Economic Cooperation and Development Observer*, no. 158, 8–12.
Pempel, T.J. 1992. "Of Dragons and Development." *Journal of Public Policy* 12: 1.
Polsby, Nelson. 1984. *Policy Innovation in America*. New Haven: Yale University Press.
Prais, S.J. 1989. "How Europe Would See the New British Initiative for Standardising Vocational Qualifications." *National Institute Economic Review*, London, 129: 52–54.
Pressman, Jeffrey, and Aaron Wildavsky. 1974. *Implementation*. Berkeley: University of California Press.
Przeworski, Adam, and Henry Teune. 1970. *The Logic of Comparative Social Inquiry*. New York: John Wiley.
Richardson, J.J., ed. 1982. *Policy Styles in Western Europe*. London: George Allen & Unwin.
Ricketts, Martin, and Edward Shoesmith. 1990. *British Economic Opinion: A Survey of a Thousand Economists*. London: Institute of Economic Affairs.
Riggs, Fred W. 1988. "The Survival of Presidentialism in America: Para-Constitutional Practices." *International Political Science Review* 9(4): 247–78.
Robertson, David Brian. 1991. "Political Conflict and Lesson-Drawing." *Journal of Public Policy* 11 (1): 55–78.
Rogers, Everett M. 1983. *The Diffusion of Innovations*. 3d ed. New York: Free Press.
Rose, Richard. 1972. "The Market for Policy Indicators." In *Social Indicators and Social Policy*, edited by A. Shonfield and S. Shaw, 119–41. London: Heinemann.
———, ed. 1974. *Lessons From America*. New York: Halsted/ Wiley.
———. 1982. *The Territorial Dimension in Government: Understanding the United Kingdom*. Chatham, N.J.: Chatham House.
———. 1983. "Electoral Systems and Constitutions. In *Democracy and Elections*, edited by V. Bogdanor and D.E. Butler, 20–45. Cambridge: Cambridge University Press; and in *Estudios Politicos (Nuova Epoca)*, no. 34, 69–106.
———. 1984. *Understanding Big Government*. Beverly Hills, Calif.: Sage.
———. 1985a. "The Programme Approach to the Growth of Government." *British Journal of Political Science* 15(1): 1–18.
———. 1985b. "From Government at the Centre to Nationwide Government." In *Centre-Periphery Relations in Western Europe*, edited by Y. Meny and Vincent Wright, 13–32. London: George Allen & Unwin.

———. 1987a. "The Political Appraisal of Employment Policies." *Journal of Public Policy* 7(3): 285–306.
———. 1987b. "Steering the Ship of State: One Tiller but Two Pairs of Hands." *British Journal of Political Science* 17(4): 409–33.
———. 1988a. "Comparative Policy Analysis: The Program Approach." In *Comparing Pluralist Democracies*, edited by Mattei Dogan, 219–41. Boulder, Colo.: Westview Press.
———. 1988b. "The Growth of Government Organizations: Do We Count the Number or Weigh the Programs?" In *Organizing Governance, Governing Organizations*, edited by C. Campbell and B. Guy Peters, 99–128. Pittsburgh: University of Pittsburgh Press.
———. 1990a. "La Presidencia al servicio del Publica." *Reforma Administrativa: Informe del Presidente de la Republica*. Bogota, Colombia: Government Printing Office, vol. 13, 165–96.
———. 1990b. "Inheritance before Choice." *Journal of Theoretical Politics* 2(3): 263–91.
———. 1991a. "Comparing Forms of Comparative Analysis." *Political Studies* 39(3): 446–62.
———. 1991b. "Is American Public Policy Exceptional?" In *Is America Different?* edited by Byron Shafer, 187–229. New York: Oxford University Press.
———. 1991c. "Prospective Evaluation through Comparative Analysis: Youth Training in a Time-Space Perspective." In *International Comparisons of Vocational Education and Training*, edited by Paul Ryan, 68–92. London: Falmer Press.
———, ed. 1991d. "Lesson-Drawing Across Nations." A special issue of *Journal of Public Policy* 11(1): 1–131.
———. 1991e. *The Postmodern President: George Bush Meets the World*. 2d ed. Chatham, N.J.: Chatham House.
———. 1992. "Escaping from Absolute Dissatisfaction: A Trial-and-Error Model of Change in Eastern Europe." *Journal of Theoretical Politics* 4 (4): 371–93.
Rose, Richard, and Philip L. Davies. Forthcoming. *Inheritance before Choice in Public Policy*. New Haven: Yale University Press.
Rose, Richard, and Edward C. Page. 1990. "Action in Adversity: Responses to Unemployment in Britain and Germany." *West European Politics* 13(4): 66–84.
Rose, Richard, and Rei Shiratori, eds. 1986. *The Welfare State East and West*. New York: Oxford University Press.
Rose, Richard, and Ezra Suleiman, eds. 1980. *Presidents and Prime Ministers*. Washington D.C.: American Enterprise Institute.
Rose, Richard, and Günter Wignanek. 1990. *Training without Trainers?*

Avoiding the Supply-Side Bottleneck. London: Anglo-German Foundation.

Sabatier, Paul A. 1988. "An Advocacy Coalition Framework of Policy Change and the Role of Policy-Oriented Learning Therein." *Policy Sciences* 21(2): 129–68.

Sabatier, Paul A., and David Whiteman. 1985. "Legislative Decision-Making and Substantive Policy Information: Models of Information Flow." *Legislative Studies Quarterly* 10(3): 395–422.

Sartori, Giovanni, ed. 1984. *Social Science Concepts.* Beverly Hills, Calif.: Sage.

Savage, Robert L. 1978. "Policy Innovativeness as a Trait of American States." *Journal of Politics* 40(2): 212–24.

———. 1985. "Diffusion Research Traditions and the Spread of Policy Innovation in a Federal System." *Publius* 15(4): 1–28.

Schmid, Günther, and Bernd Reissert. 1988. "Do Institutions Make a Difference? Financing Systems of Labour Market Policy." *Journal of Public Policy* 8(2): 125–50.

Schmitter, P.C., and G. Lehmbruch, eds. 1980. *Trends toward Corporatist Intermediation.* Beverly Hills, Calif.: Sage.

Schumpeter, Joseph A. 1946. "The American Economy in the Interwar Period." *American Economic Review* 36, supplement: 1–10.

———. 1952. *Capitalism, Socialism and Democracy.* 4th ed. London: George Allen and Unwin.

Shapiro, Margaret. 1988. "Empire of the Sun," *Washington Post Weekly Edition*, 31 October.

Simon, Herbert A. 1947. *Administrative Behavior.* New York: Macmillan.

———. 1969. *The Sciences of the Artificial.* Cambridge, Mass.: MIT Press.

———. 1978. "Rationality as Process and as Product of Thought." *American Economic Review* 68(2): 1–16.

———. 1979. "Rational Decision Making in Business Organizations." *American Economic Review* 69(4): 493–513.

Sivard, Ruth L. 1987. *World Military and Social Expenditures 1987/88.* 12th ed. Washington D.C.: World Priorities.

Solow, Robert M. 1985. "Economic History and Economics." *American Economic Review* 75(2): 328–31.

Staple, Greg. 1990. *The Global Telecommunication Traffic Boom.* London: International Institute of Communications.

Steinbach, Carol. 1990. *Innovations in State and Local Government.* New York: Ford Foundation.

Stoetzel, Jean. 1983. *Les Valeurs du Temps Présent.* Paris: Presses Universitaire de France.

Stokes, Donald. 1963. "Spatial Models of Party Competition." *American Political Science Review* 57: 368–77.

Studlar, Donley T. 1987. "Policy Convergence: Political Economy in the United States and Britain." In *Political Economy*, edited by J.L. Waltman and D.T. Studlar, 3–15. Jackson: University Press of Mississippi.

Summers, Lawrence H. 1991. "Lessons of Reform for the Baltics." Paper presented to Hudson Institute Conference on Baltic Economic Reform, Indianapolis, 29 October.

Taagepera, Rein, and M.S. Shugart. 1989. *Seats and Votes: The Effects and Determinants of Electoral Systems.* New Haven: Yale University Press.

Tait, Alan A. 1988. *Value-Added Tax: International Practice and Problems.* Washington D.C.: International Monetary Fund.

———. 1990. "IMF Advice on Fiscal Policy." In *Public Finance and Steady Economic Growth*, edited by Gerold Krause-Junk, 38–52. The Hague: Foundation Journal Public Finance.

Tanzi, Vito. 1987. "A Review of Major Tax Policy Missions in Developing Countries." In *The Relevance of Public Finance for Policymaking*, edited by Hans M. van de Kar and Barbara L. Wolfe, 225–36. Detroit: Wayne State University Press.

Thompson, George (Sir). 1961. *The Inspiration of Science.* London: Oxford University Press.

Tocqueville, Alexis de. 1954 edition. *Democracy in America.* 2 volumes. New York: Vintage Books.

United Nations Development Program. 1991. *Human Development Report 1991.* New York: Oxford University Press.

Vogel, David. 1987. "The Comparative Study of Environmental Policy." In *Comparative Policy Research: Learning from Experience*, edited by M. Dierkes, H.N. Weiler, and A.B. Antal, 99–170. Aldershot: Gower.

Walker, Jack L. 1969. "The Diffusion of Innovation among American States." *American Political Science Review* 63(3): 880–99.

Waltman, Jerold L. 1980. *Copying Other Nations' Policies: Two American Case Studies.* Cambridge, Mass.: Schenkman.

Weiner, Myron, and Ergun Ozbudun. 1987. *Competitive Elections in Developing Countries.* Durham, N.C.: Duke University Press.

Weiss, Carol H. 1972. *Evaluation Research: Methods of Assessing Program Effectiveness.* Englewood Cliffs, N.J.: Prentice-Hall.

Westney, Eleanor. 1987. *Innovation and Imitation: The Transfer of Western Organizational Patterns to Meiji Japan.* Cambridge, Mass.: Harvard University Press.

White, Stephen, ed. 1990. "Elections in Eastern Europe." *Electoral Studies* special issue, 9(4): 275–366.

Wildavsky, Aaron. 1979. *Speaking Truth to Power: The Art and Craft of Policy Analysis.* Boston: Little, Brown.

———. 1988a. *Searching for Safety.* New Brunswick, N.J.: Transaction Books.

———. 1988b. *The New Politics of the Budgetary Process.* Boston: Little, Brown.

Wolman, Harold. 1990. "Understanding Cross-National Policy Transfers: The Case of Britain and the U.S." Paper presented at the annual meeting of the American Political Science Association meeting, San Francisco.

Wright, Deil S. 1988. *Understanding Intergovernmental Relations.* Pacific Grove, Calif.: Brooks/Cole.

———. 1990. "Policy Shifts in the Politics and Administration of Intergovernmental Relations, 1930s–1990s." *The Annals,* May, 60–72.

Wright, Deil S., and F. Ted Hebert. 1990. "Evolving Personal and Policy Profiles of State Administrators." Paper presented at the meeting of the Southern Political Science Association, Atlanta, 9–11 November.

Index

Abortion, 131
Adaptation, 30
Agency for International Development, 44
AIDS, 83
Air University, xvi
Alabama, xv, 155
Alaska, 98, 100, 120
Albany, 100
Almond, Gabriel, xvi
Analogies, 26, 84
Anglo-German Foundation, xiv
Aristotle, x
Arizona, 103, 107
Arkansas, 98ff, 148
Athens, x, 95
Atlanta, 99
Australia, 97, 109
Austria, 109

Belgium, 6, 43, 109
Bennett, Colin, xv
Berlin Wall, xv, 18
Blockage, total, 34, 38ff
Bonn, 55
Boston, 55
Braybrooke, David, 88f
Britain, xiv, 6, 9, 22, 27, 43, 47, 75, 106, 109, 114f, 125
Bruno, Michael, 37
Brussels, 55, 70, 155
Budgeting, 28, 89f, 130
Bulgaria, 112
Bush, George, 110
Bushong, Robert, xvi

California, 23, 25, 98, 101f, 107, 148
Camdessus, Michel, 20
Canada, 5f, 10f, 22, 55, 61, 75, 96f, 100, 109, 114, 151
Carter, Jimmy, xiii
Catching up, 17, 111ff, 156
Chad, 130
Cholera, 48
Civil rights, 90, 155f
Civil servants, 55ff, 127
Clemens, Elisabeth, 56
Clinton, Bill, xii, 139, 154
Colombia, xiii
Complexity, 131ff, 149
Concepts, 13, 16, 21
Conley, Ray, xvi
Connecticut, 99f
Consensus, 9, 37, 141
Constitutions, 124, 138
Contingencies of lessons, 14f, 86ff, 118–42, 145ff
Convergence, 36
Cooper, Richard N., 48
Copying, 30
Cosmopolitans, 51
Courts, 97, 122, 127, 138. *See also* Law
Creativity, 29ff
Cuba, 100
Cyclical problems, 87f
Cyert, Richard, 51
Czechoslovakia, 111ff

Data protection programs, 7f, 69, 128f

Defense, 88, 124
Delaware, 100
Dempster, M.A.H., 89
Denmark, 7, 70, 96, 109
Detroit, 2, 155
Developing nations, 6, 15, 19, 70f
Diffusion studies, 15
Dissatisfaction, 3, 50ff, 57ff, 90
Dresden, 156

Eastern European nations, 17, 31, 46, 111f, 156
Economic resources, 96ff, 127, 130f, 148
Economics, 10ff, 19, 35, 61f, 66f, 112f
Education, 65, 73, 115f, 150
Elected officials, 53ff
Elections, 31, 39, 45, 61, 153
Embassies, 125
Empires, 138
Energy consumption, 132
Enthoven, Alain C., ix
Environment, 10f, 60, 66f
Epidemiology, 65
Eskimos, 120
Estonia, 112
Etheredge, Lloyd, xvi
Ethiopia, 130
European Community (EC), 6, 9f, 15, 32, 41, 55, 60, 64, 69f, 105ff, 110, 129, 139f, 149f, 155

Index

Evaluating lessons, 32ff, 45ff, 71ff
Experience, 1f, 4, 18f, 33
Experts, 10, 14, 19, 55ff, 64ff, 112f, 125, 149f

Faith, unbounded, 93ff
Feasibility, 45f
Federalism, x, 34, 64, 68, 74, 97ff, 124, 127, 137, 151
Feedback, 63
Fenno, Richard F., Jr., 53
Fesler, James W., 77f
Finland, 109
Florida, 100f
Ford car, 34
Ford Foundation, 122
Founding Fathers, 95
France, 6f, 9, 43, 75, 96, 106, 108, 114, 125
Freedom of Information Act, 22, 81
Fungibility, 34ff, 42, 46, 121, 124

Gandhi, Mahatma, 155
Generations, 152
George, Alexander, xvi
Georgia, 99
Germany, xiv, 3, 6, 9, 43, 70, 75, 88, 96f, 101, 108f, 111, 113ff, 125, 138, 150, 154ff
Gestalt theories, 40
Gibean, Victor, xvi
Glaser, William A., xvi
Gorbachev, Mikhail, ix
Greece, 109, 111, 113

Haig, Alexander, 85
Hall, Peter A., xvi
Hamburg, 107
Hanke, Stephen, 35
Harmonization of laws, 129
Hawaii, 100
Health policy, 8, 61, 65, 74f, 123f
Heclo, Hugh, 59, 147

Hedberg, Bo, 52
Heraclitus, 38
History, uses and abuses of past, 1, 21, 62, 78ff, 84ff
Hitler, Adolf, 85
Hoberg, George, xv
Hong Kong, 108
Howard, Michael, 79
Hungary, 111ff
Hussein, Saddam, 85
Hybrid programs, 31

IBM, 36
Ideology, 81, 96, 101ff
Illinois, 100
Implementation, 91
Incrementalism, 86ff, 135
Infant mortality, 74
Inflation, 20, 59f, 67
Inheritance, 38f, 78, 136
Innovation, 24
Inspiration, 31
Instability, 47ff
Institutions, 26, 122ff, 147f
Interdependence, 6, 10f, 107, 136ff, 150f
International Monetary Fund (IMF), 64, 70f, 95, 105
Interstate compacts, 100
Iowa, 100f
Ireland, 70, 98, 109
Iron Curtain, 41, 106
Isolation, xi, 40ff
Italy, 55, 70, 106, 109, 114

Japan, xii, 6, 27, 41ff, 46, 55, 61, 74f, 88, 100, 108f, 127, 151, 154f
Johnson, Lyndon B., 60

Kansas, 100
Katmandu, 95
Kennedy, John F., 155
Kentucky, 100
Keynes, J.M., 87
Kincaid, John, 107

King, Martin Luther, Jr., 155
Koop, C. Everett, 9
Kuwait, 85

Language, 2, 115
Law, 8, 66f, 122, 128,
League tables, 24, 73ff
Leapfrogging, 106f
Leipzig, 156
Lewis, Sinclair, 143
Life expectancy, 104
Limerick, 107
Lindblom, C.E., 88f
Literacy, 104f
Lithuania, 112
Liverpool, 107
Local government, 2, 5, 23, 28, 42, 137, 151
London, 55
Los Angeles, 55
Louisiana, 5, 99

McDonalds, 36
Mackenzie, W.J.M., xvi
Majone, Giandomenico, xv
Major, John, 47, 94, 109
Malaysia, 108
March, J.G., 123, 136
Marmor, Theodore, xvi
Marxism-Leninism, 106
Massachusetts, 23, 101f
Maxims, 20f
May, E.R., 86
Media, 154
Medicare, 61, 78
Medicine as diagnostic science, 13
Mediterranean, 10
Mercedes, 36
Mexico, 96, 100, 107, 151
Michigan, 101f
Minnesota, 5, 101f, 129
Mississippi, 98, 148,
Missouri, 56
Models, 13, 29, 33
Montgomery, Alabama, xvi, 155

173

Munich, 85

Napoleon, 125
Nepal, 95
Netherlands, 6f, 106, 109
Neustadt, Richard E., 86
New Deal, xii, 153
New Hampshire, 99
New Jersey, 100f
New Mexico, 99, 107
New York, 25, 55, 98ff, 148
New York City, 100, 129
New Zealand, 98, 109
Nixon, Richard, 82
North American free trade area, 151
North Atlantic Treaty Organization (NATO), 78
North Dakota, 99
Norway, 96, 109

O'Neill, Thomas P., Jr. (Tip), 53
Olsen, J.P., 123, 136
Organization for Economic Cooperation and Development (OECD), 69, 107, 109, 111, 130, 147, 149
Organizations, 52f
Organs, trade in, 67

Pacific Northwest, 129
Paradigm shift, 25f
Paris, 55
Path dependence, 39
Pennsylvania, 100
Persian Gulf war, 85
Pluralization, 36
Poland, 111f
Policy entrepreneurs, 56f
Policymakers, locals and cosmopolitans, 51ff
Poll tax, 94
Portugal, 109, 111, 113
Poverty, 60
Precedent, 83

Predictability, 134
Presidency, U.S., xiii, 54, 154ff
Pressure group officials, 56
Prime ministers, xiii
Propinquity, 25, 96, 99ff
Programs defined, 21ff
Prospective evaluation, 32–34, 114–17
Prussia, 43, 125

Quebec, 5

Race relations, 39f, 90
Ravenna, 107
Reagan, Ronald, 5, 78, 81, 110, 154
Reissert, Bernd, xv
Resources: money, law, officials, 14, 98, 104f, 127ff,
Rhode Island, 98
Riddle, Ann, xvi
Robertson, David Brian, xv
Rokkan, Stein, xvi
Romania, 112
Roosevelt, Eleanor, 118
Routines, 58f, 72

Sabatier, Paul, xvi
Sachs, Geoffrey, 37
Sartori, Giovanni, 12
Saskatchewan, 5
Satisficing, 58, 72
Scandinavia, 108f, 129
Schmid, Günther, xv
Schumpeter, Joseph, 77
Scientism, 92f
Scots law, 128
Searching for lessons, 27ff, 50–76, 95–117. *See also* Space, Time
Segregation, xii, 155
Shop opening hours, 132
Siberia, 100
Simon, Herbert, xvi, 11f, 58f

Simplicity of programs, 132ff, 149
Singapore, 108, 149
Slovenia, 112
Social Security, 78, 89
Solow, Robert, 37
Somalia, 130
Sony Walkman, 36
South Korea, 108, 149
Soviet Union, 113f, 150
Space, searching across, 1, 5ff, 16, 21, 28, 32, 62ff, 68ff, 95–117
Spain, xiii, 98, 109, 111, 113
Speculation, intellectual, 14ff, 90ff, 112, 114
Standardization, 36, 122
State government, 7, 21, 28, 42, 97ff, 127, 137, 151
Statistical information, 69
Stevenson, Adlai, 118
Stewart, William, xvi
Substitutability, 124
Summers, Lawrence, 35, 156
Switzerland, 4, 109
Symbol, 27

Taiwan, 108, 149
Taxation, 6, 32f, 67, 94, 99, 130, 136
Technology, 3, 7f
Telephone, 3f, 105f,
Tennessee, 100
Terence, 95
Territorial justice, 151
Texas, 100, 103
Thatcher, Margaret, 47, 81, 94, 109
Thompson, Sir George, 12
Thucydides, 78
Thurn, Georg, xv
Time, searching across, 1, 5ff, 16, 21, 26ff, 32, 38, 47, 61, 71ff, 77–94, 110ff, 143ff, 152ff
Tocqueville, Alexis de, 12, 154
Tools, 4, 12f, 21

Index

Trade unions, 67
Transferability of programs, 21ff, 36, 42, 46. *See also* Fungibility
Transportation, 124, 154
Trial and error, 63
Trudeau, Pierre, 138
Turkey, 113

Ukraine, 112
Unemployment, xiii, 9f, 59f
Uniqueness, 38, 119ff
United Nations, 104ff

Values, political, 15, 22, 39, 44ff, 60, 101ff, 107ff, 140ff, 151
Vietnam, 85
Virginia, 103
Vocational education and training, 115f, 129, 131, 139

Wage-price controls, 67, 126
Wallace, George, 155
War on Poverty, 153
Watergate, 81

West Virginia, 98
Wignanek, Günter, xv
Wildavsky, Aaron, xvi, 89
Will, political, 93ff
Wilson, Harold, 153
Wisconsin, 100, 129
Wissenschaftszentrum Berlin, xiv
World Bank, 35, 70f, 105, 156
Wyoming, 99

Zapf, Wolfgang, xv

About the Author

Richard Rose brings to the study of lesson-drawing a great breadth of knowledge about politics and public policy in the United States and Europe. A native of St. Louis, he took an undergraduate degree in comparative literature at Johns Hopkins University and, after further education at the London School of Economics and the *St. Louis Post-Dispatch*, his doctorate at Oxford. For a quarter of a century Rose has pioneered the study of comparative public policy from a base at the University of Strathclyde in Scotland, where he is the founder and director of the Centre for the Study of Public Policy.

Rose has viewed American local and state politics at first hand as a reporter and lobbyist, and Washington close at hand as a visiting scholar at the Brookings Institution, the American Enterprise Institute, the Woodrow Wilson International Center, and the International Monetary Fund. Internationally, he has been a consultant to the World Bank, the OECD, the Paul Lazarsfeld Society, and is a Fellow of the British Academy.

In the course of his academic career Rose has held appointments as a visiting professor at Stanford University, Johns Hopkins University, the University of Illinois, the European University Institute in Florence, the Wissenschaftszentrum, Berlin, and the Central European University, Prague. In 1990 he gave the Ransone lectures at the University of Alabama on the theme of lesson-drawing. Currently he is directing a twelve-nation research program on mass response to the transition from state to market in post-Communist Eastern Europe.

Rose is internationally known for writing clear and vivid prose joining concepts, empirical data, and apt examples drawn from the past and present. He has addressed academic and public policy audiences on five continents. Translations from his one hundred books and articles have appeared in Chinese, French, German, Greek, Hebrew, Italian, Japanese, Norwegian, Polish, Portuguese, Russian, Spanish, and Swedish.